T0182498

Artificial Intelligence

in Byte-sized Chunks

Artificial Intelligence

in Byte-sized Chunks

Peter J. Bentley

Michael O'Mara Books Limited

First published in Great Britain in 2024 by
Michael O'Mara Books Limited
9 Lion Yard
Tremadoc Road
London SW4 7NQ

A CIP catalogue record for this book is available from the British Library.

Papers used by Michael O'Mara Books Limited are natural, recyclable products made from wood grown in sustainable forests. The manufacturing processes conform to the environmental regulations of the country of origin.

ISBN: 978-1-78929-656-3 in hardback print format
ISBN: 978-1-78929-681-5 in trade paperback print format
ISBN: 978-1-78929-658-7 in ebook format

1 2 3 4 5 6 7 8 9 10

Cover design by Barbara Ward
Designed and typeset by Claire Cater
Illustrations by David Rojas Márquez
Printed and bound by CPI Group (UK) Ltd, Croydon, CR0 4YY

www.mombooks.com

Contents

Introduction

We are amazing. We are living, embodied organisms, designed by billions of years of evolution to be able to survive in our complex environments. Our brains, in isolation, are the most complex structures we know about in the universe. Our bodies are also astonishingly complex, with billions of cells performing their choreographed dances as defined by the tiny molecular instructions of our genes. And we are not alone. All living organisms, big and small, have been subjected to the forces of evolution for the same duration as we have. They are all astonishingly clever in their own ways at surviving in their respective niches.

Biological brains are so advanced that they puzzle us. How can a collection of wet cells that somehow fire little electrical signals at each other do something as undefinable as think? How can they reason? Or plan? How can they enable us to move around? How can they enable you to read these words and understand them? What's going on right now inside your skull as your billions of neurons think about themselves thinking?

Brains also tempt us. Cleverness is just so appealing. We love a clever pet that recognizes us and interacts with us. We marvel at a clever bird that can mimic any sound that it hears. We are fascinated by any clever technology that somehow learns about us or about its world and changes itself in response.

It's perhaps no surprise that we've spent a lot of effort making such clever technologies. After all, what could be better than an autonomous vehicle that parks itself – or even drives us to our destination? Or a smart home that optimizes its internal environment to suit our needs, while minimizing the costs? Who wouldn't want a smart security system that monitors our safety and automatically alerts the authorities if intruders are detected? Would you really refuse a smart health system that monitors you and helps detect any medical issues early enough that they can be cured?

There are so many smart technological solutions today that help us in our daily lives. We live in an age of science fiction come true. I have a smart dishwasher and washing machine that both detect their respective contents and automatically adjust water usage and cleaning programs to save energy. I have a robot vacuum cleaner that cleans my floors, and I can see that it doesn't miss any spots, as I might. (It can't do the stairs though.) I have a smart heating system that heats only the zone of the house I'm in, and that adjusts its program depending on the weather outside as well as the temperature inside. I have a smart home that detects where I am and, based on the time of the sunrise and sunset, controls lighting automatically. It also knows if I leave and can prime the alarm and external cameras, which automatically detect people and record their movements, and can even detect if a parcel is left and alert me. I have a smart TV, phone, car, watch and various other gadgets that I can actually talk to. They detect it's me from my voice and can answer my questions or find a show I might like to see, or a product I'm currently looking for. You might have a smart fridge or kitchen that looks at your groceries and auto-suggests recipes based on what you have and their use-by dates – and automatically orders new groceries when you run short. You might have a smart solar-power system that powers your home and recharges the car at optimal times, providing surplus energy back to the grid for everyone else to use. (I don't have those yet!) I do have a smart camera that figures out what to focus on and processes the image so that it looks as good as possible. And I've lost count of how many smart software applications I have that can clean up images further or invent entirely new ones, make music, identify people in photos, write computer code and a hundred other things. I'm a computer scientist, so perhaps I see some of this tech a bit sooner than most, but be assured that if you don't have it yet, you probably will soon.

This is just a tiny fraction of artificial intelligence today. Somehow our fascination with intelligence (plus no lack of hubris) has resulted in countless technological marvels. And these marvels are just getting better and better. After decades of struggling, with many AIs not quite able to do what we hoped, recent attempts have started to work astonishingly well. When a company can go from an invention to a valuation of a billion dollars in ten months, you know AI is not just working, it's making a lot of people very, very excited. From about 2015 onwards, major corporations around the world have invested tens of billions of dollars to have their own AI systems in the hope that this will give them that extra edge. AI has come of age. Today it works well enough that it's an integral part of many everyday products.

But a world where we have working AI pervasive throughout our technology also means something else. It means that we do not always know if an image or piece of music or even a passage of text is written by a human or not. This blurring of creative authorship challenges our traditional notions of creativity and authenticity in the digital age. And in case you just noticed a change of style, that previous sentence was generated by an AI, when asked to add to the first two sentences in this paragraph. If I wanted to, I could ask the same AI to finish writing this Introduction. It would do a pretty good job, too. Give it my other books to ingest and it would even closely duplicate my writing style. (I can't because there's a new clause in my contract that says I cannot use an AI to write this book!)

This is the world we now find ourselves living in. It's a world where truth and fiction may be troublesome to distinguish. It's a world where our children can ask an AI to do all their homework for them, be it maths, science, English, history, art or music. We must learn to cope with the potential for our own data to be gobbled up by some AI and incorporated into a new solution produced by that AI without us ever knowing about it. And we must deal with the fact that as much as all these smart technologies are helping us, they may also be invading our privacy by recording every detail about our lives and using that data for applications unknown to us.

AI in the form of smart technology is here and likely to stay. But is it really intelligent? It might feel as though it can understand our words and respond with intelligent, reasoned replies. But what kind of intelligence do these different kinds of AI have? How do they really work, anyway?

In this book I'll explain artificial intelligence (in bite-sized chunks). I'll give some insights into those clever researchers who figured out how to make inanimate machines seem smart. But most importantly, I'll tell the story of AI by focusing on the AIs themselves. Together we'll see what each AI can do – and what it can't. We'll discover how they work, and how decades of improvements have led to the extraordinarily complex AIs that we have today. We can't look at every AI, but I'll pick a few significant and interesting examples to show how we progressed. And in the words of an AI itself: 'As we delve into the past, present and potential future of AI, we'll uncover the intricate dance between human ingenuity and the ever-evolving realm of artificial intelligence.'

Or would you prefer a different ending to this Introduction? Try this one by the same AI:

'And fear not, dear reader, for this journey through the realm of AI will be as enlightening as it is accessible, guiding you through the intricate pathways of artificial minds with clarity and simplicity.'

Could I have put it better? Well, I'd like to think so. Judge for yourself!

1950-1960

The Birth of Artificial Intelligence

A New Era

The Second World War brought devastation and horrific suffering for millions of people. But like all wars, it acted as a catalyst for rapid technological advancement. By the late 1940s and early 1950s, we had the first programmable computers – albeit the size of a large room. We also had a huge amount of surplus army components, no longer needed for the battlefields. The great thinkers of their generation were no longer needed to build exotic machines for calculating how to decrypt enemy messages or how to build the most effective weaponry. They were free to consider more fundamental questions. And with the mental health of many soldiers deeply affected by their experiences in the war through what became known as post-traumatic stress disorder (PTSD), there were plenty of mysteries relating to the brain for the psychologists and neurobiologists.

So as the towns and cities were being rebuilt around them, it was a new post-war environment of optimism in which researchers began to think seriously about the brain and intelligence. Not a new topic, and many great minds in past decades had written much on the subject. But now things were different, for computer technology had been invented. Using these new high-tech machines, the war-tested ingenuity of these talented scientists could surely solve this problem. After all, how complex could the brain really be?

Two-Neuron Artificial Brains

Neurobiologist William Grey Walter, based at the University of Bristol and a pioneer of the electroencephalograph (EEG machine) was one of the scientists who tried to understand intelligence in this new optimistic environment. After his experience in studying the human brain using the EEG, he had an idea. Instead of just studying brains, perhaps if you could *make* a brain then you could understand it better.

Grey Walter used pieces of old alarm clocks and army surplus materials to build two mechanical tortoises called Elmer and Elsie: autonomous battery-operated robots that used a rotating light sensor on the top to detect bright lights and move towards them. They also had touch sensors on the body so that if they bumped into an obstacle they would move away from it. Grey Walter likened their brains to two sensory neurons: one for light, one for touch. Surprisingly, despite such minimal brains, he discovered they showed remarkably complex behaviours, randomly 'exploring' their environments and finding their own way back to their 'hutches' to charge. He added a light to the nose of one, which turned off when the light sensor received sufficient signal, and placed the robot in front of a mirror so that it could see its own light. The robot jiggled about and flashed the light as if excited to see itself. This fascinated Grey Walter, who wrote:

The creature therefore lingers before a mirror, flickering, twittering, and jigging like a clumsy Narcissus. The behaviour of a creature thus engaged with its own reflection is quite specific, and on a purely empirical basis, if it were observed in an animal, might be accepted as evidence of some degree of self-awareness.

Elmer and Elsie

(ELectroMechanical Robots, Light Sensitive

Late 1940s

Overview: Mechanical tortoises that moved towards light and away from obstacles

Strengths: Pioneering autonomous robots with the equivalent of two neurons for a brain

Weaknesses: Attracted to women's legs

Ethical Issues: None

Developer: William Grey Walter

It was not the only lifelike behaviour shown by Elmer and Elsie. Apparently they also had a distinct attraction towards women's legs. The 1940s nylon stockings reflected light in just the right way to make them irresistible to the robots.

Grey Walter continued his experiments for some years, later creating a more advanced tortoise robot called Cora (Conditional Reflex Analogue), which was designed to learn how to associate a whistle with a light, inspired by Ivan Pavlov's experiments with dogs that were trained to salivate at the sound of a bell. Although Cora started life as a robot much like Elmer and Elsie, eventually Grey Walter performed 'surgery' and removed the specific learning circuits so he could study this part of the electronic brain on its own.

Cybernetics

When he wasn't constructing strange mechanical menageries or using EEG to study the human brain, Grey Walter was also a regular at the Ratio Club. This was an informal dinner club frequented by leading neurobiologists, mathematicians, physicists, psychologists and engineers. The name Ratio was coined because of its meaning in Latin: logic, reason, judgement. It forms the root of words such as rational, ratify, rate. The club was founded by John Bates, a neurologist who was likely inspired by the recent book written by American mathematician and philosopher Norbert Wiener, *Cybernetics: Or Control and Communication in the Animal and the Machine.* The twenty-one members soon became known as the core of the British cybernetics movement. They were all prominent members of their respective fields and all made significant breakthroughs in their careers.

Cybernetics was the first formal study of intelligence, by considering cybernetic loops – the idea that an animal or a machine exhibits behaviour because its sensors detect something, which affects its controller. The controller performs an action in response that then results in an effect to some external system: its environment. The change is then detected by the sensors, which affect the controller, and so on, in a loop. Cybernetics was the first attempt at understanding intelligence in this way, and those such as Grey Walter who tried to build cybernetic systems were making the first electronic artificial intelligences.

Alan Turing

Amongst the members of the Ratio Club was a genius mathematician, fresh from helping to decode German encrypted messages during the Second World War at Bletchley Park. By the 1950s, Alan Turing was already a high achiever in his field. He was the first to define a mathematical notion of what computers were. He also proved they would always have some limitations – for example, a computer cannot always figure out if its program will halt or not. Because of this we discovered that some problems are not computable – they just cannot be calculated by a computer. Turing helped design and program some of the first computers in the world. He and his colleague David Champernowne, an economic statistician, who had helped provide Churchill with vital data during the war, also wrote one of the first ever chess-playing AI programs, called Turochamp.

As well as being an AI, Turochamp is generally considered to be one of the first ever computer games to be developed. But it suffered from one fatal flaw – it was too complex for any computer at the time to run. Although in 1952 it 'played' a full game of chess with computer scientist Alick Glennie (the inventor of Autocode, the first ever compiler, which turns human-readable computer language into native machine code executed by the processor), it

Turochamp

(combination of surnames Turing and Champernowne)

1948

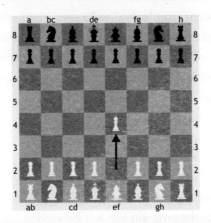

Overview: Early computer program to play chess

Strengths: One of the first ever programs that could play a simple game of chess

Weaknesses: Too complex to be run on contemporary computers

Ethical Issues: None

Developers: Alan Turing and David Champernowne

required Turing to perform the role of computer and hand-calculate the program's execution, taking about thirty minutes per move.

Turochamp worked by keeping a record of the current chessboard and accepting the opponent's moves as input. It would then consider all legal moves that it could make in response, followed by all responses that the opponent could make, followed by any significant move that could be made, such as capture of a piece worth less than the piece taking it. It assigned scores to each potential move and then used a *minimax* algorithm to decide which move to make. This is a classic AI heuristic (rule of thumb) that says if you can assign scores to your own moves and the moves of your opponent, and look ahead a few moves, then you should pick the moves that result in the best score for yourself to *maximize* your chances of winning while *minimizing* the chances of your opponent winning. (A year later, in 1949, another computer pioneer named Claude Shannon built a remarkable relay-packed machine that could play end games of chess with up to six pieces, and also used the minimax algorithm; by 1959, computer scientist Arthur Samuel had used similar ideas in his checkers-playing AI.)

In 1952, the so-called 'paper machine' Turochamp lost to Glennie in twenty-nine moves. Exactly sixty years later, this game was analysed as the program was being recreated for an anniversary event (the Alan Turing Centenary Conference). The researchers discovered to their surprise that Turing had probably cheated in the original game, not playing moves suggested by the program when they seemed suboptimal. When the recreated program played a game of chess against world champion Garry Kasparov in 2012, it lost in sixteen moves. Disappointing perhaps, but given its extremely limited thought process, only looking ahead a couple of moves, this early AI did pretty well. Even without Turing around to give it a helping hand.

Turing Test

Alan Turing had strong beliefs about the likely future capabilities of computers. He predicted that people would 'speak of machines thinking' by the end of the century. He also believed that by then we would be able to program computers such that when chatting to them we would not be able to tell if they were human or machine.

Turing claimed that 'an average interrogator will not have more than a 70 per cent chance of making the right identification after five minutes of questioning.' He called this the Imitation Game (which also became the title of a biographical movie made about Turing in 2014). Today we refer to it as the Turing Test.

Turing died aged only forty-one in 1954. But his work, and specifically the Turing Test, became hugely influential and has been hotly debated ever since. Thousands of AI researchers were inspired by this test, which seemed almost like a challenge: if you can make an AI that chats as realistically as a human, then maybe you have made a machine that thinks. Such 'chatbots', as they eventually became known, became an important focus for many AI researchers in the years that followed. The Turing Test also became a topic of some irritation for others.

Universal Constructor

In what turned out to be some of his last work, published in 1952, Turing recognized that there is more than one kind of intelligence. He investigated morphogenesis, or how we develop into complex organisms from a single cell. This clever process somehow controls our cells as they act like little computers executing intricate genetic programs written into our DNA. Turing showed how some clever equations that mimic how chemicals can react with each other are able to spontaneously form patterns.

In the USA, there were many important pioneers of computing also thinking about intelligence. Perhaps the most famous of them all was mathematical genius John von Neumann, who helped create the world's first programmable computers, and wrote a highly influential report about it, with the result that all subsequent computers were said to follow the 'von Neumann' architecture.

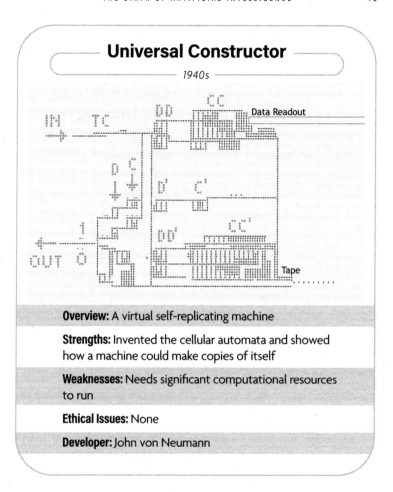

Universal Constructor

1940s

Data Readout

Tape

Overview: A virtual self-replicating machine

Strengths: Invented the cellular automata and showed how a machine could make copies of itself

Weaknesses: Needs significant computational resources to run

Ethical Issues: None

Developer: John von Neumann

Like Turing, by the late 1940s, von Neumann had turned his mind to new forms of intelligent behaviour. While Turing had realized that biological development used its own kind of cleverness, von Neumann looked at an even earlier stage in biology: how does life make copies of itself? He considered an idea that even today remains science fiction: imagine if we had a clever machine that could make itself. Not only that – what if that self-replicating machine could grow in complexity like living systems? Would it then evolve, forming species and complex life? This kind of cleverness would be smart technology unlike anything we've ever seen before.

Von Neumann couldn't build such a machine as there was not (and still is not) any physical tech existing that would enable us to achieve this goal. In 1949, the early computers were also too simple to run a simulation of his idea. So, like Turing's chess AI, he had to design his 'universal constructor' machine on paper. It was a remarkable piece of engineering even so. Von Neumann first created the idea of a cellular automaton – a grid of 'cells' where each could take one of twenty-nine states, and the state of each cell depends on the state of its neighbouring cells. His design was extremely clever, for his self-replicating machine would use a string of instructions to make a new copy, and then copy those instructions over to that new machine so that it could then make a copy of itself, and so on. This was perhaps inspired by the recent discovery that DNA might be responsible for carrying genetic information needed to define living organisms. But it preceded the discovery of the structure of DNA by Watson and Crick (and Rosalind Franklin) by several years – von Neumann was ahead of his time. The insight was important: separate the instructions from the machine as our DNA is separated from the cell, and those instructions could then mutate and evolve, resulting in the construction of more and more complex life. Von Neumann was not able to complete this work before his death, but decades later, scientists continued working on the idea. It was not until the following century that computer scientists were able to show von Neumann's designs working on a modern computer.

Dartmouth Conference

For most researchers, the idea of machines making themselves and growing like living organisms was beyond them (and still is today).

But the idea of computers that could think like people? That was something they could get their teeth into.

The early 1950s became a heyday for this unnamed field. Some called it cybernetics. Others preferred information processing, or automata theory. But in 1955, a group of pioneering American scientists proposed the first conference where everyone should meet to discuss this emerging field of research. It would take place in Dartmouth College, in the USA. In their proposal, they named the field *Artificial Intelligence*.

The event took place in 1956, consisting of eight weeks of talks and discussions amongst many of the leading pioneers at the time. The event formed the catalyst for the field of artificial intelligence and laid the foundations for many of the key ideas that were to dominate the field for decades to follow. It was a time of great excitement and optimism, with many new AIs being created that followed different principles.

Dynamic Programming

Intelligence can mean many things. One definition of intelligence is the capability to find good solutions to problems. If you're clever you can figure out the answer to a tricky problem. Computer scientists and mathematicians tend to be a bit literal about things, so when they talk about *finding* they really mean it. They ask the computer to search a virtual space comprising all possible solutions to the problem and locate the best solution, like finding buried treasure in a massive, complicated landscape. In later years, search and optimization algorithms were to become increasingly important parts of AI as they gave computers the ability to find good solutions to difficult problems (optimization can also be regarded as search). But as early as the 1950s, mathematician Richard Bellman invented a method that became the cornerstone of countless AIs and programming languages of the future. He called it dynamic programming. In a nutshell, it's a trick for solving a difficult problem by breaking it down into smaller pieces, and then reducing the number of times those pieces need to be calculated.

Imagine we want a computer to generate the Fibonacci sequence: 0, 1, 1, 2, 3, 5, 8, 13, 21, 34 … where each number is made by adding the two previous numbers.

A naive approach would be to use a recursive function that calls itself each time to figure out how the previous numbers were constructed. So to calculate the number after 34 it needs to know the previous two numbers, but to know those, it needs to know the previous numbers before them, and so on, until it gets back to the start. It's recalculating everything from the ground up, for every new number.

A method using dynamic programming understands that this problem has building blocks that get reused. Once we've calculated a couple of numbers, we can just remember them as the last two, which we use to calculate the next one. The current number and the previous number then are stored as the last two, which we can use to calculate the next one, and so on.

Just a simple trick, but dynamic programming methods allow computers to find solutions to problems massively more efficiently, taking far less time in their search. It's been used in smart software for everything from bioinformatics to economics ever since.

Logical Thinking

Dynamic programming was not the only idea to be invented in this era. In the 1950s, one of the most attractive ideas was based on logic and reasoning. From the early days, some mathematicians and computer scientists preferred this approach in AI, for they felt a logical artificial mind would be more predictable and make it possible to prove what the AI could and could not do.

Logic Theorist

1955

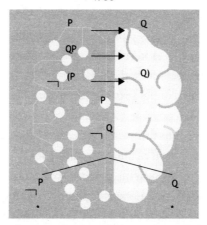

Overview: First program that could prove theorems as well as a mathematician

Strengths: Had a major impact on AI and cognitive psychology, established symbolic AI

Weaknesses: Was limited to the domain of logic

Ethical Issues: None

Developers: Allen Newell, Herbert A. Simon and John Clifford Shaw

The Logic Theorist was one of the methods demonstrated at the Dartmouth Conference, although it only received a lukewarm reception at the time. It had been conceived the year before by American computer scientist Allen Newell and Herbert Simon, a political scientist who was to later win the Nobel Prize for his theory of bounded rationality (the idea that rational people typically make satisfactory decisions, but those decisions are not always the best possible choices). Programmer 'Cliff' Shaw was asked to develop the program.

The Logic Theorist built on the idea of using search to find solutions to problems – in this case, finding a valid proof that led from a logical hypothesis to a proposition. A simple example might be the hypothesis that if it rains then the pavement becomes wet, and if the pavement is wet then the pavement is slippery. If we say that today it is raining, then we can deduce that the pavement will be slippery. It's possible to represent very complex ideas and mathematics in various forms of logic, and so having an automatic theorem prover was seen as quite revolutionary.

This AI program worked by using three clever tricks that quickly became fundamental to AI and computer science as a whole. First, similar to dynamic programming, the Logic Theorist relied on the idea that *search* could be used to find the right proof in a massive landscape of alternatives. It considered the landscape to be like a tree: the hypothesis was the root and countless different branches grew from it, each a possible logical statement deducible from the hypothesis. Somewhere in the massive tree lay the proposition, and so the Logic Theorist had to search the tree to find it. The problem was that the more complex the hypothesis, the more gigantic the tree became. In fact, it grew exponentially, which meant there was no way it could be searched exhaustively – even a computer would take much too long. Instead of breaking the problem into smaller steps as dynamic programming might, the second innovation comprised 'rules of thumb' which Newell and Simon called 'heuristics'. Like a tree surgeon, these would prune away any branches of the tree that looked bad, leaving far less tree to search. To make it all work, their third innovation was a special new computer language based on processing lists of symbols.

Logic lay at the heart of this AI and it performed extremely well, proving thirty-eight of the first fifty-two theorems in chapter 2 of the well-known foundational maths book *Principia Mathematica* by Alfred Whitehead and Bertrand Russell. One of its proofs was more compact and elegant than the original in the book, with Russell responding 'with delight' when shown by Simon. Before long, a lot of people became very excited by this AI. While it worked in the domain of logic, it was built to solve problems like a human. Significantly, it allowed concepts to be represented by symbols, and then it could reason about the world using these symbols. (For example, 'if it's raining and not windy then I'll use an umbrella' might become U -> R ∧ ~W.) The researchers became so excited they began making somewhat grandiose predictions. Simon claimed at the time:

It is not my aim to surprise or shock you – but the simplest way I can summarize is to say that there are now in the world machines that can think, that can learn and that can create. Moreover, their ability to do these things is going to increase rapidly until – in a visible future – the range of problems they can handle will be coextensive with the range to which the human mind has been applied.

Herbert Simon (1958)

From these ideas, and perhaps inspired by some of these excitable comments, symbolic processing became one of the cornerstones of AI and had a major impact on cognitive scientists for decades. Two years later, the same team extended the work to make another more general AI, which they called the General Problem Solver (GPS). This could now perform simple planning, for example playing simple games.

AI with Common Sense

John McCarthy was a young assistant professor in 1955 when he joined other researchers in proposing the Dartmouth Conference. By 1958, he had moved to MIT as a research fellow and was performing AI research in the area of list processing, in a very similar vein to the work of Newell and Simon. McCarthy took his work even further, creating a more useful list-processing language which became known as LISP. This language enabled programmers to process lists of symbols with computers far more easily, and was to be used for decades in subsequent AI research.

One of McCarthy's first demonstrations of the use of list processing was in his AI, conceived with colleague Marvin Minsky, which he called the Advice Taker. Described in 1959, McCarthy's idea was for the AI to be able to process symbols and manipulate language as though operating using 'common sense'. He contrasted this with the approach taken in the Logic Theorist, which used heuristics hidden inside the AI and followed predefined rules for manipulating logic. In the Advice Taker, all of its behaviours would be defined in the list-processing language itself. It would be given new information which would be stored as carefully formatted lists of symbols, and then it would be able to deduce new facts and consequences based on the knowledge it had gained. Describing the work, McCarthy wrote: 'Our ultimate objective is to make programs that learn from their experience as effectively as humans do.'

He also described how he wanted the AI to operate more like a human than a machine. We program computers using precise imperative sentences: do this, do that. McCarthy and Minsky were imagining an AI where you describe the situation and provide a simpler instruction about what is required.

The Advice Taker was never built, but McCarthy's vision of how we might prompt AIs eventually came true some sixty years later, with the advent of Large Language Models (chapter 111).

Advice Taker
1958

1. atd.desk) — can (go (desk,car,walking))

2. at(l,car) - can(go (home, airport. driving))

3. did(go(deskcar,walkmg)) — at(I, car)

4. did(go (home,airport,driving)) -* at(I, airport)

5. canachult (atd.desk), go (desk, car, walking) , at(l.car))

6. canachult(at(l, car), go(home, airport,driving) , at(l, airport))

7. canachult(at(l, desk), program!'go (desk, car,walking), go (home, airport, driving)), - at (I,airport))

8. do(go (desk, car, walking))

Overview: Used logic and list processing to represent information and perform common-sense reasoning

Strengths: Pioneered the idea of an AI building a knowledge base of information and using it to reason

Weaknesses: Never actually implemented in a computer

Ethical Issues: None

Developers: John McCarthy and Marvin Minsky

Neural Networks

A very different kind of idea had been created by neurophysiologist Warren McCulloch and logician Walter Pitts using logic, albeit 'logical calculus', back in 1943. In their work they described a mathematical notion of a neuron. Although highly simplified compared to the neurons in your head, it had sufficient complexity to do some interesting things. They described a neuron as a weighted sum of inputs, pushed through a 'transition function' to produce an output. They called it a *perceptron*.

Think of a perceptron like a major road tunnel under a river. There are multiple roads converging at the entrance to the tunnel, and on each road there are speed limits that slow or speed up the traffic. There's a traffic light at the other end of the tunnel. It's either green, letting the traffic flow out onwards to its destination, or it's red, stopping the traffic. The light is controlled by a transition function, which basically says if the traffic is flowing into the tunnel fast enough, turn the light green, otherwise keep it red. You can imagine there are various scenarios: if all the input roads have speed limits that restrict their flows, then the sum of all the traffic will be low or zero, and the traffic light will remain red. If we make one road have no limit and it can speed through, then the traffic light may switch to green. If we constantly change the speed limits, then the light will switch from red to green depending on the sum total of the traffic flowing. This is how the perceptron works. The inputs (roads) have weights (speed limits). The neuron output (output road) is either on or off (has green or red traffic light) depending on a function of the sum of the weighted inputs (total traffic flowing in). This is intended to model a biological neuron, which has multiple inputs (dendrites) and one output (axon). It fires electrical signals out of the axon depending on the signals coming in via the dendrites.

One perceptron on its own may not sound very interesting, but use a bunch of them together and you have a different kind of AI. Marvin Minsky was another of the young scientists who put together the proposal for the Dartmouth Conference. But before Minsky rose to his eventual fame as one of the fathers of AI, he started as a grad student doing an interesting project. Back in 1951, Minsky

SNARC
(Stochastic Neural Analog Reinforcement Calculator)
1952

Overview: First ever neural network machine, made from 40 Hebb synapses – used components from the autopilot of a B-24

Strengths: Demonstrated self-learning in a connectionist neural network

Weaknesses: Very unreliable, frequently broke down

Ethical Issues: None

Developers: Marvin Minsky, Dean Edmonds and George Armitage Miller

was a mathematics grad student at Princeton University, USA. He had become interested in neurons after reading about perceptrons, and also neuropsychologist Donald Hebb's book *The Organization of Behavior*, and wrote a letter to American psychologist George Armitage Miller (regarded as one of the founders of cognitive science, or the study of intelligent behaviour). Miller obtained some funding and Minsky plus Dean Edmonds, a talented physics grad student at Princeton, got to work. Their aim was to build a network of artificial neurons, using vacuum tubes. It was a highly unusual machine comprising forty neurons (or more properly Hebb synapses) wired together. Each neuron used a capacitor to briefly store electricity and act like a short-term memory – whether the neuron was active or not. It used a potentiometer (like the rotary volume control on a hi-fi) to behave as long-term memory – the weights on the inputs. When given the task of learning to navigate a maze, the neurons adjusted themselves so that the potentiometer settings stored information, in the same way that the weights of neurons are adjusted in neural networks today to learn data, as we'll see later. The forty different volume controls were adjusted by this bizarre machine itself using electric motors, a mechanical chain (much like a bicycle chain) and a clutch from a B-24 bomber aircraft.

By 1952, they demonstrated the SNARC solving a maze, with a virtual rat running around randomly, better choices slowly reinforced by adjusting the neuron weights. This was following 'Hebbian learning' that states that if neurons are simultaneously active and are associated with some event, then they should have a stronger connection between them, often stated as 'cells that fire together, wire together'. SNARC kept its rat running until it successfully learned to reach an exit. Due to a few bugs they also realized they sometimes had multiple virtual rats running around, influencing each other as they tried to solve the maze. All held in the mind of the forty-neuron SNARC machine, and visualized using arrays of little light bulbs, which lit up to show the location of the rats.

This was the first known attempt at creating a self-learning artificial neural network, and although the idea was to become hotly debated in later years, partly because of Minsky himself, neural network technology would become a firm favourite for AIs.

Perceptive AIs

Minsky's SNARC was the first neural network inspired by the perceptron. But the first Perceptron AI was implemented in 1957 in software on an IBM 704 (the first ever mass-produced digital mainframe computer). And in 1958, the full-blown Mark 1 Perceptron machine was built by American psychologist Frank Rosenblatt and his team.

It was a remarkable machine, built at Cornell and funded by the US Office of Naval Research. It was designed to perform image recognition, with a 20x20 array of photocells as input, connected to the 'association unit' neurons which had fixed weights, connected to eight output or 'response' neurons, each of which had weights encoded with potentiometers like SNARC. Instead of the SNARC's complex chain and clutch approach, each potentiometer was connected directly to an electric motor that could twiddle the volume controls independently. The output neurons could then classify images: the combination of which neurons were on and which were off was used to describe what kind of image was being seen at the input. The neural network could be trained by showing it an input and adjusting the weights of the neurons (potentiometers) until the desired output was produced by the output neurons. This learning was performed automatically by the machine, with various types of visual patterns used for training (such distinguishing the letters E and X, or diamonds and squares) projected on to the photosensors as patterns of dots using a slide projector. The images were presented multiple times during training, and were transformed by moving, rotating or changing the size of the 'stimulus', so that different neurons had a chance

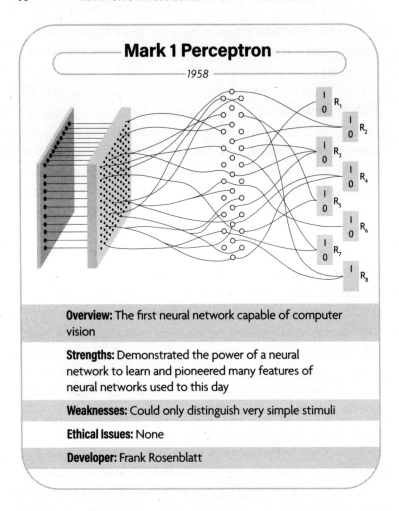

Mark 1 Perceptron

1958

Overview: The first neural network capable of computer vision

Strengths: Demonstrated the power of a neural network to learn and pioneered many features of neural networks used to this day

Weaknesses: Could only distinguish very simple stimuli

Ethical Issues: None

Developer: Frank Rosenblatt

to 'experience' and learn the pattern. Once trained, the neural network could be shown an image and correctly classify it: this is a square, not a diamond.

Like Simon, Rosenblatt was not afraid to speak with the media. In 1958, at around the same time Simon was making grand claims about the Logic Theorist, Rosenblatt provided sufficiently juicy quotes that *The New York Times* wrote:

The Navy revealed the embryo of an electronic computer today that it expects will be able to walk, talk, see, write, reproduce itself and be conscious of its existence. Later perceptrons will be able to recognize people and call out their names and instantly translate speech [...] it was predicted.

The scientific community – especially Minsky – was not amused. The researchers found such obvious hype not only distasteful, but wholly unprofessional. But nevertheless, the publicity had an effect – new researchers started working on neural networks in earnest. Now the field of artificial intelligence had two horses running at the front of the race: the 'symbolist' logical AIs and the 'connectionist' neural network AIs.

CHAPTER 001

1960-1970

Over-Optimism

The Times They Are a-Changin'

The 1960s was a period of change for the world. Memories of war were being overtaken by a new generation of post-war youths who wanted something different from the preoccupations of their parents. Movements advocating new civil rights grew: the legalization of abortion, sex and racial anti-discrimination. A counterculture of psychedelic colours, peace, rock and roll music grew. Times were changing and scientists were not immune to changing sentiment. Filmed interviews and newspaper articles started featuring AI researchers and their incredible inventions. And the predictions from these scientists – many already well established and prominent in their fields – became less and less plausible:

'I'm convinced that machines can and will think in our lifetime.'
Oliver Selfridge, 1961

'I confidently expect that within a matter of ten or fifteen years something will emerge from the laboratory which is not too far from the robot of science fiction fame.'

Claude Shannon, 1961

'Machines will be capable, within twenty years, of doing any work that a man can do.'

Herbert Simon, 1965

'Within a generation, I am convinced, few compartments of intellect will remain outside the machine's realm – the problem of creating "artificial intelligence" will be substantially solved.'

Marvin Minsky, 1967

Looking back, we now know that these visions were wildly over-optimistic. But in the swinging sixties, these scientists were seeing computers achieve feats of intelligence that seemed almost unbelievable to them. This was a time of breakthroughs, of fiction becoming fact. They were becoming caught up in the excitement of the time – and they would not be the last to do so.

Expert AIs

At around the same time that McCarthy proposed the Advice Taker, a young man called James Slagle was awarded a prize of $500 (today equivalent to more than $6,000) from President Eisenhower for his outstanding work as a blind student – he achieved the highest grade in his university. Slagle went on to MIT to do a PhD under the supervision of Marvin Minsky, who together with McCarthy had initiated what would eventually become MIT's Computer Science and AI Laboratory. (In 1963 McCarthy moved institutions and founded the Stanford Artificial Intelligence Laboratory, SAIL.) Slagle's PhD expanded on the ideas seen in Logic Theorist and Advice Taker. He wrote an AI that solved symbolic integration problems. By the time he was finished in 1961, his SAINT (symbolic automatic integrator) AI was able to solve fifty-two out of fifty-four MIT freshman final examination questions on the

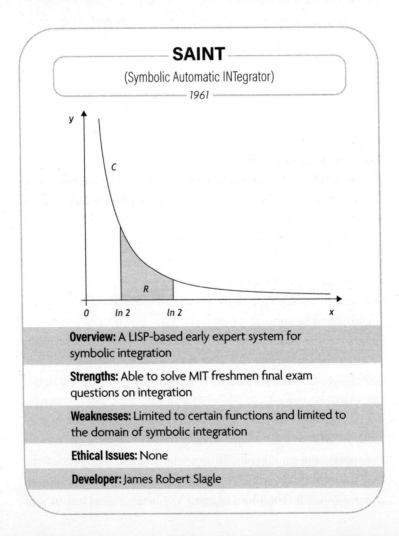

SAINT

(Symbolic Automatic INTegrator)

1961

Overview: A LISP-based early expert system for symbolic integration

Strengths: Able to solve MIT freshmen final exam questions on integration

Weaknesses: Limited to certain functions and limited to the domain of symbolic integration

Ethical Issues: None

Developer: James Robert Slagle

topic. A remarkable achievement for a blind student when the IBM 7090 computer that he used was still a large machine filling a room and needed punched cards to program it – indeed, his AI took specially formatted punched cards as input and printed out its answer on paper.

Symbolic integration is a kind of calculus. It's the tricky kind, where you have to transform one maths function into another to find the antiderivative, or integral, of that function. In differential calculus, a derivative refers to the rate at which something changes. Take the derivative of a function and you can figure out the rate of change for that function. Integral is the opposite – it takes the derivative and gives the original function (often visualized as the area under the graph). It's tricky stuff because there are so many rules to remember, so questions on integration are still normal for maths students to this day.

The SAINT AI was written in McCarthy's new language, LISP. He combined many of the ideas of the time, embedding knowledge in the form of heuristics and custom algorithms to transform functions appropriately, and using pruning of 'goal trees' to reduce the complexity of the problem for the computer as it worked through its task. While much of its domain-specific knowledge was tangled up with the algorithms to solve the problem, SAINT is considered by some to be the first *expert system* AI. It was an AI that knew a lot about a specific subject, and when asked a question (what is the integral of this or that) it could consult its internal knowledge, follow some heuristics and provide a correct answer.

Life on Mars

Expert systems would soon become the new golden child of AI. Dendral, one of the earliest and most successful true expert systems, was developed in 1965 by a team of highly talented scientists and their team at Stanford University. Joshua Lederberg was a famous molecular biologist who had just won the Nobel Prize in 1958 for his discovery that bacteria could mutate and exchange their genes with each other. In the early 1960s he began working with chemist Carl Djerassi – also famous in his field, for he had helped create the first oral contraceptive pill. Joshua was fascinated with computers and wondered if they could help suggest new chemical compounds that might be alternative organic compounds to those seen on Earth. More specifically, given a mass spectrometry analysis of a sample, could the computer reverse-engineer the result and suggest the chemical composition of the sample? There was a very practical and profound application. Lederberg had a contract with NASA, with the aim of creating a technology that could make sense of samples taken by a future exploration robot on Mars. If the robot could scoop up samples, analyse them with a mass spectrometer, and send the result back to Earth, then could you deduce whether the sample contained organic compounds? Could you detect life on Mars?

They enlisted computer programmers Edward Feigenbaum, Georgia L. Sutherland and Bruce Buchanan to help with the project. They (and their research assistants and grad students) wrote the first version of Dendral (Dendritic Algorithm) in LISP. It would create graphs corresponding to possible chemical compounds that matched the desired mass spectrum, and using heuristics would prune away chemically implausible structures. Heuristic-Dendral led to further versions such as Meta-Dendral and CONGEN that could plan, generate and test chemical graphs satisfying a set of constraints, using a built-in knowledge base of chemical and graph information. Dendral and its many offspring continued into the 1970s and early 1980s, with new expert systems such as MYCIN (which identified bacterial infections and recommended appropriate antibiotics), MOLGEN (which helped plan

Dendral

(Dendritic Algorithm)

1961

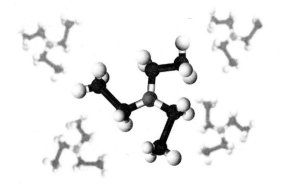

Overview: A LISP-based early expert system for suggesting new chemical compounds

Strengths: A revolutionary way for computers to provide expert-level knowledge and assistance on a specific topic

Weaknesses: Not easy to set up – needed years of work from many experts and programmers

Ethical Issues: None

Developers: Joshua Lederberg, Carl Djerassi, Edward Feigenbaum, Georgia L. Sutherland, Bruce Buchanan and many others

laboratory experiments in molecular genetics), PROSPECTOR (which aided geologists in mineral exploration for the US Geological Survey), XCON (an expert configurator for computer systems), and STEAMER (which helped evaluate new AI technology for training systems) all created from this beginning.

Natural Language Understanding

Robert K Lindsay was one of the computer scientists to work on Dendral in later years. In 1961 he had a slightly different interest – using computers to understand written English. Natural language processing, as it became known, was a new way to approach artificial intelligence. Scientists and engineers had attempted automatic translation for some years already, with limited success as they tried to codify every possible translation into a set of rules; not something you can do very well with the limited memories and processing of the computers back in the 1950s and 1960s. Lindsay had another idea. His AI, to which he gave the unfortunate name of SAD (sentence diagrammer), accepted a simplified version of English, known as Basic English, designed for learning English as a foreign language. Simple English sentences were provided as input and he used the list-processing language IPL (as used in the Logic Theorist by Simon and Newell, who were his mentors) to store information derived from them, using its built-in knowledge of vocabulary, idioms, dates and places to form a syntactic map. This would then be analysed by the second part of the AI, called SAM (semantic analyser). SAM focused on family relationships and constructed family trees based on the English input to SAD. So if SAD was given a sentence such as:

```
James had two children, a boy called Harry and a girl
called Susan. Susan was married with no children.
Harry had children, called Tom and Dick. James was
married to Edna. His father was called John.
```

SAM would output the family tree looking a bit like this:

```
            John - ?
               |
          James - Edna
            /      \
   Harry - ?      Susan - ?
     /    \
   Tom    Dick
```

This was a first: an AI that could build a model of a topic (the family tree) from nothing but English sentences. Even the first Large Language Model AIs created in the early 2020s struggled to perform this task as well as this early AI. Lindsay went to start one of the first graduate courses on artificial intelligence, at the University of Texas in Austin. He devoted his entire career to the pursuit of 'understanding understanding', as he put it.

Meanwhile, in the MIT AI Group of Minsky, student Daniel Bobrow was beginning his PhD research. It was a great time to be at MIT because a huge grant of $2 million was awarded by the Defense Advanced Research Projects Agency (DARPA) for Project MAC – research into Mathematics and Computation. This award was under the direction of 'Johnny Appleseed', J C R Licklider – the same visionary who would fund work into graphical user interfaces and the ARPANET, later to become the Internet. The AI Group became incorporated into Project MAC and benefitted tremendously from the funding.

Bobrow was another PhD student of Minsky, and another to build an AI using LISP. Inspired by the work of Lindsay, he also decided to tackle NLP. But he wanted to go further than have a computer only build an internal model. Could a computer

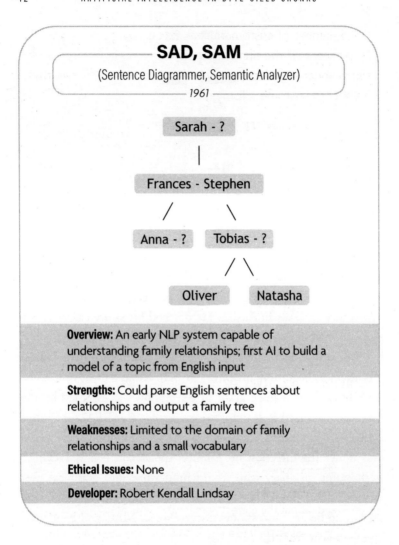

SAD, SAM

(Sentence Diagrammer, Semantic Analyzer)

— *1961* —

Sarah - ?

Frances - Stephen

Anna - ?   Tobias - ?

Oliver   Natasha

Overview: An early NLP system capable of understanding family relationships; first AI to build a model of a topic from English input

Strengths: Could parse English sentences about relationships and output a family tree

Weaknesses: Limited to the domain of family relationships and a small vocabulary

Ethical Issues: None

Developer: Robert Kendall Lindsay

understand an English sentence well enough to respond with an answer to a question? Bobrow decided to focus on algebra story problems. These are the kinds of things your maths teacher at school might ask you (and this is an actual example from Bobrow's thesis):

If the number of customers Tom gets is twice the square of 20 per cent of the number of advertisements he runs, and the number of advertisements he runs is 45, what is the number of customers Tom gets?

STUDENT

1964

```
PLUS      P1 PLUS P2      (PLUS, P1*, P2*)

MINUS     P1 MINUS P2     (PLUS, P1*,(MINUS, P2*))

          MINUS P2        (MINUS P2*)

DIVBY     P1 DIVBY P2     (QUOTIENT P1* P2*)
```

Overview: An early NLP system which could answer algebra stories

Strengths: Could parse English sentences about maths and output the correct numerical answer

Weaknesses: Limited to the domain of algebra stories and a small vocabulary

Ethical Issues: None

Developer: Daniel Bobrow

Bobrow's AI STUDENT used its built-in knowledge of language and maths and substituted words with equations until it could perform the desired calculation, outputting the answer as a number:

```
(THE EQUATIONS TO BE SOLVED ARE)

(EQUAL X00001 (NUMBER OF CUSTOMERS TOM (GETS / VERB)) )

(EQUAL (NUMBER OF ADVERTISEMENTS (HE / PRO) RUNS) 45 )

(EQUAL (NUMBER OF CUSTOMERS TOM (GETS / VERB) ) (TIMES
2 (EXPT (TIMES .2000 (NUMBER OF ADVERTISEMENTS (HE /
PRO) RUNS)) 2)))

(THE NUMBER OF CUSTOMERS TOM GETS IS 162)
```

Bobrow completed his PhD on the topic in 1964. He went on to create his own AI department in MIT's spin-out R&D company BBN and pioneered many advances in the field. He never lost his love of language, always enjoying word games and puns.

Look Who's Talking

I talked with a new therapist the other day. It didn't go so well.

```
> Hello, I am Eliza. I'll be your therapist today.

* I'm feeling happy today

> How long have you been feeling happy today?

* All day!

> OK... 'I'm feeling happy today'. Tell me more.

* That sounds sarcastic

> I see. Let's try another topic and we will come back
to that issue later.
```

* Well now I'm not feeling so happy

> Do you enjoy being not feeling so happy?

* Uh... not really!

> I'm not sure I understand you fully.

* Are you a qualified therapist?

> Would you prefer if I were not a qualified therapist?

I'm not sure I'll go back. But this therapist was ELIZA, built in 1966, and the conversation is not too bad for one of the first ever chatterbots, or chatbots as they became known. It wouldn't pass the Turing Test – it's very clear that it is not human. Eliza is clever, for it can reply with some set phrases such as 'why do you think that?' or 'that's an interesting response' or 'tell me more' when it has no other suitable response for your input. But for those performing a Turing Test, the constant deflections soon make it apparent that your conversation is with a machine, not a thinking human.

ELIZA was the creation of Joseph Weizenbaum, a computer scientist and sometimes seditious colleague of Minsky at MIT, in 1966. Weizenbaum had been born to Jewish parents in Berlin and emigrated to the USA in 1936. After working on several early computers and helping to create the first computer system to read magnetically encoded fonts on the bottom of cheques, he took a position at MIT in 1964. He decided he would take the work on natural language processing in a new direction, building a program designed to provide the illusion of conversing with us, but with no intention of trying to have the computer understand our words. He deliberately created a program that could learn new 'scripts' so that it could add to its vocabulary and create new responses, all controlled by a simple set of heuristics, implemented using Weizenbaum's own list-processing language. When parodying

ELIZA (DOCTOR)

1966

Overview: The first chatbot

Strengths: Could give a simple illusion of a conversation, by playing the part of a psychologist

Weaknesses: Designed to be a parody of communication and had no internal model with which to understand sentences

Ethical Issues: Users felt their conversations with Eliza should be private and unavailable to the developer

Developer: Joseph Weizenbaum

a 'Rogerian psychologist' it went by the name of DOCTOR. To Weizenbaum's surprise, his program elicited unexpected responses from those who used it. People chatted to it as though it were human. They shared their secrets and problems with it. They enjoyed the experience. 'What I had not realized is that extremely short exposures to a relatively simple computer program could induce powerful delusional thinking in quite normal people,' he later wrote.

Indeed, ELIZA was soon being held up as being the future of psychology or providing a general solution to the problem of computer understanding of natural language. Weizenbaum was shocked. He attempted to clarify that no general solution was possible, for understanding of language depends on shared contextual frameworks. For example, we both have experienced apples before, so we understand each other if we talk about an apple. A computer cannot experience an apple. He argued that even people may not share such frameworks perfectly, so we are also not examples of a general solution: if I have experienced a durian fruit before and you have not, our communication about it may be more difficult as we have less shared understanding. Computers have almost no experience of the world that we have, and so to expect them to converse with us and have any form of understanding is naive. While people may have fooled themselves that ELIZA was a 'person' they could share their thoughts with, this was pure anthropomorphism. The machine was designed to be a parody of conversation!

Logical Thought

Despite Weizenbaum's growing misgivings, work on AI continued with a strong focus on the use of symbolic logic and list processing. Thomas Evans was another MIT PhD student to try his hand at creating an AI. By 1964 he was showing off ANALOGY – another heuristic-driven LISP-based AI that could take geometric shapes as input (defined by their coordinates), figure out which shapes were inside which, figure out a set of rules from those relationships, and apply them to a new shape, with the result that it could solve geometric problems as used in IQ tests: C is to what as A is to B?

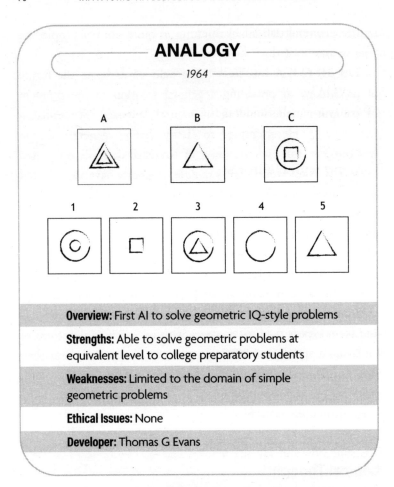

ANALOGY

1964

Overview: First AI to solve geometric IQ-style problems

Strengths: Able to solve geometric problems at equivalent level to college preparatory students

Weaknesses: Limited to the domain of simple geometric problems

Ethical Issues: None

Developer: Thomas G Evans

There seemed to be no end to the successes of this symbolic logic-based AI. By 1968, yet another AI had been created by another of Minsky's students. MACSYMA (Project MAC's SYmbolic MAnipulator) took the ideas of the Logic Theorist and ran with them. Joel Moses not only did his PhD on the topic, he helped take the program to customers. MACSYMA was eventually able to perform a huge variety of mathematical operations, from integration to general relativity. It was developed at MIT until 1982 and then commercialized by licensing it to a software company called Symbolics (which has the claim to fame of registering the first ever dot-com address in the world: symbolics.com). By 1999, MACSYMA was released under GNL (general public release) and to this day it remains under maintenance by enthusiasts.

Thinking with Neurons

But symbolic logic wasn't the only way to make an AI. Research on neural networks also continued unabated in the 1960s. Rosenblatt's Perceptron inspired ADALINE by Bernard Widrow, professor of electrical engineering at Stanford, and his PhD student Ted Hoff. ADALINE worked in a similar way to the Perceptron, with weighted inputs being summed and pushed through a simple transition function to give an output. It also had the idea of a bias – a bit like one extra road with a permanently large amount of traffic and its own speed limit converging on to all those other roads, using our previous analogy. This means the output was now the sum of weighted inputs plus a constant (the bias), pushed through the transition function. Modern neural networks also use the idea of a bias in exactly this way – the weights of the normal inputs determine how quickly the neuron will fire, while the bias can control the threshold at which the neuron fires.

ADALINE was created in electronics using components called memristors which, as the name suggests, could remember their states – handy to store the values of the neuron weights. It was also important because it used a way of automatically updating the weights of its inputs in order to minimize the error at the output. ADALINE used a method which we now call stochastic gradient descent – a very popular method used in machine learning today. In optimization we wish to find the optimum value for a maths function, for example $f(x) = x^*x$ is smallest when $x = 0$. This simple

ADALINE

1960

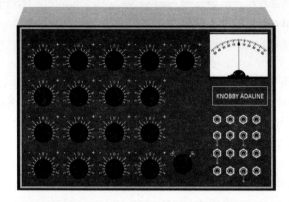

Overview: Early neural network implemented with memristors

Strengths: Introduced ideas of bias and stochastic gradient descent

Weaknesses: Only able to learn simple linearly separable patterns

Ethical Issues: None

Developers: Bernard Widrow and Marcian 'Ted' Hoff

optimization algorithm randomly samples a function (like trying random values for x) to figure out its slope (the function gets smaller as x gets smaller), then follows the slope down (the size of steps being set by the 'learning rate') until it finds the lowest point, or minimum. That's the optimal value, and for neural networks, that means it's the value for all the weights such that the error between neuron output and desired output is zero. (Gradient descent is the non-random version of the same algorithm – when you can figure out the gradient of the function directly, you don't need to randomly sample it.)

ADALINE was able to learn simple patterns input using a 4x4 bank of toggle switches, such as distinguishing between the letter *T* and *J*. MADALINE was created a few years later and used the same neurons but in three layers: input, 'hidden' and output, just like a modern neural network. It used different learning rules for each layer, but one was later found to be equivalent to backpropagation – which was later to become a fundamental notion in neural networks.

Widrow continued his research in electrical engineering at Stanford for decades. Ted Hoff was to follow a different path, joining Intel in 1968 as the twelfth employee in the role 'manager of applications research'. He soon suggested a new way of building computers – instead of creating them from multiple different circuits all wired together, he suggested that a 'universal processor' could be made as one unit. This was the start of the microprocessor – the first large-scale integration of transistors on one chip, which led to a subsequent revolution in computers in the following decades, and the creation of our modern technological world.

Deeper Learning

A single perceptron (or a single-layer perceptron network) is basically when we connect the input directly to one side of the network and the output is what comes out the other side. So if we're teaching the neural network to recognize letters, we'd put pixel values of ones and zeros to the inputs and we'd look at the output of the neuron to 'see what it thought'. But perceptrons like this are just thresholding the sum of weighted inputs (plus that bias), so they are limited in what they can distinguish. It turns out that they can only distinguish linearly separable inputs. That means that if you were to graph the inputs as a set of points, the neural network can only do the equivalent of drawing a straight line to separate them into different classes. If the inputs are more complicated and a straight line cannot separate them, then this simple neural network cannot learn to distinguish, or classify, the data correctly.

Researchers realized this limitation very early on. The solution? Make the neural networks *deeper*. Instead of a single layer with input and output connected to the same neuron(s), use multi-layer perceptrons (MLPs) where inputs are fed into an input layer of neurons, *their* outputs feed into a 'hidden layer', and their outputs feed into an output layer, with their outputs then being used to see what the network thinks the answer is. Each neuron (or 'node') is connected to every neuron in the following layer, with every connection having a weight that needs to be set when training the network. This is a three-layer MLP, but add more layers in the middle and you can increase the depth of the neural network. It was shown some thirty years later that you only need an MLP of two layers to create a universal approximator – the neural network can approximate any function. We use maths functions to model almost everything (from movement to shape to commerce) – so the neural network can approximate almost everything, too.

A Ukrainian mathematician called Alexey Grigorevich Ivakhnenko demonstrated a kind of multi-layer neural network in 1965, called the Group Method of Data Handling, training his neural network layer by layer. But the first more recognizable deep neural network was created in 1967 by Japanese researcher Shun'ichi Amari. He used stochastic gradient descent to enable his neural networks to adjust their own weights across the whole network and he showed that his network was able to classify non-linearly separable patterns. Shun'ichi Amari continued to perform research into neural networks and brain science for his entire working life, making several important contributions to the field.

Thinking Matchboxes

In the early 1960s, computers were vast expensive monoliths that were difficult to access and hard to use. Not every researcher could secure time on these rare and expensive pieces of equipment. One researcher, partly in response to a bet, found a totally unique alternative: matchboxes.

Donald Michie (known as 'Duckmouse' to his colleagues) was a British pioneer in artificial intelligence. He had been a close colleague of Alan Turing during the war, helping to decrypt German cipher codes. In addition to playing chess with Turing, Michie had been enlisted after the war by Turing to try and help recover Turing's silver bullion bars, which he had buried fearing a German invasion. Unfortunately, the areas had been redeveloped and they never recovered Turing's stash – they remain hidden in their buried hiding places to this day.

Michie had kept in touch with Turing until Turing's death, while pursuing studies in genetics. By 1958 he took a position at Edinburgh University and partly as a bet against a colleague who said it was impossible, and partly to continue Turing's concept of 'paper machines', he devised a manually operated AI made from matchboxes and glass beads. He named it MENACE (Machine Educable Noughts and Crosses Engine).

He demonstrated the machine in 1961. MENACE learned to play noughts and crosses (tic-tac-toe). It comprised 304 matchboxes, each corresponding to a specific possible game state, or unique combination of noughts and crosses on the grid. (One box for the first move corresponding to the empty grid, human plays second, then twelve boxes for the third move – because after

MENACE

Machine Educable Noughts and Crosses Engine

1961

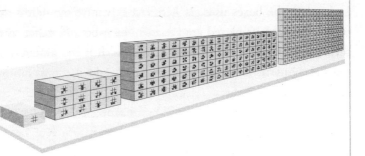

Overview: Early example of reinforcement learning, implemented first with matchboxes

Strengths: Successfully able to learn how to play noughts and crosses

Weaknesses: Limited to domain of noughts and crosses, needed to enumerate every possible move in the game

Ethical Issues: None

Developer: Donald Michie

the second move the grid may be in one of twelve states, human plays fourth, 108 boxes for the fifth move, human plays sixth, and finally 183 boxes for the final seventh move.) Inside each matchbox were up to nine different coloured glass beads, where the colour represented where MENACE could make its next move. To determine what MENACE would do, the human needed to find the right matchbox, and take out a bead at random, the colour determining the move. Pick out a red and MENACE plays its circle at the bottom middle; pick out a gold and it plays in the middle; pick out a white and it plays top left. If there's no space to move there, pick out another bead until you find a valid space. The learning part was clever: at the end of the game, the beads are updated in the boxes used. If MENACE won, three new beads of the same colour played are added to each box. If it lost, then the beads used are removed from the boxes. If it was a draw then just one bead of the same colour played is added to those boxes used. Michie called this a 'reinforcement loop'. Today we call this *reinforcement learning* in AI, and by updating the beads we are performing *credit assignment*. We're rewarding behaviours that led to better outcomes and penalizing behaviours that led to worse outcomes. By updating the beads in this way, MENACE becomes more likely to play moves that will lead to it winning the game. Indeed, usually after twenty games or so, it learnt to play so well that it couldn't be beaten.

Michie gained some notoriety for his matchbox AI and was invited by the US Office of Naval Research to Stanford. There he wrote a program based on MENACE for an IBM computer. He returned to Edinburgh and secured funding for research into machine intelligence. In 1966, he started Edinburgh University's Department of Machine Intelligence and Perception and continued to pioneer AI and robotics methods.

Meanwhile back at MIT, other game-playing AIs had been built. Mac Hack was one example, for once written in assembly language (a low-level language closer to the native language used by the computer) and not using the favourite MIT AI language of the time, LISP. Mac Hack was an enhanced version of an earlier chess-playing AI by students of McCarthy. MIT student and programmer Richard Greenblatt added fifty of his own heuristics and also used 'transposition tables' – caches of previous game positions and their respective evaluations (not unlike MENACE's matchboxes) – to speed up search of the tree of possible moves. Mac Hack was the first AI to play chess in actual tournaments. By 1967 it had gained its own USCF rating of 1510, beating real humans during its tournament games, and had an honorary membership of the United States Chess Federation.

The Chill Begins

The 1960s had been an amazing decade of progress in AI. But it was still a decade of too much hype, with exaggerated promises made by over-enthusiastic researchers. Despite the successes, people began to notice just how costly the research had been. Questions started to be asked.

The first damning report came from a related field: machine translation. Since the 1950s, linguistics and computing had attempted to automate translation, often using hard-coded rules and dictionaries. While some limited success had been achieved translating between Russian and English for scientific documents, the research had been expensive and did not live up to the early hype. A report was commissioned into progress by the US government. It was published in 1966. The Automatic Language Processing Advisory Committee, a group of seven scientists asked to gather evidence, was negative. Machine translation was less accurate and more expensive than human translation, and progress was unlikely to be fast in the field. While some recommendations for improvement were made, the findings from the report were enough to halt machine translation research entirely in the US, and reduce it severely in other countries.

Next came a book written by Marvin Minsky and MIT colleague Seymour Papert, the co-creator (with Wally Feurzeig and Cynthia Solomon) of the Logo (or Turtle) programming language widely used in teaching. Together Minsky and Papert authored *Perceptrons*, published in 1969. Their book was a theoretical study of their own simplified version of Rosenblatt's perceptions. They showed that their simplified perceptrons could not compute even some relatively simple functions, making neural networks seem rather more limited than had been thought. This was in contrast to Rosenblatt's book a decade before which had already shown the ability of these neural networks to converge and compute many forms of function. Minsky and Rosenblatt had known each other since school, having studied at the Bronx High School of Science one year apart. Minsky himself had created one of the earliest neural network AIs: the SNARC (see previous chapter). Nevertheless, Minsky's book was far from a glowing endorsement of neural networks. It caused considerable debate among academics and for many years afterwards there was a clear perception by many that Minsky and Papert had deliberately tried to stifle neural network research as they favoured their own symbolic logic-based AI.

Whether this was deliberate or not, the result was similar. Those directly working on neural networks remained relatively unaffected as they knew the criticisms in the book were largely irrelevant – using multi-layer perceptrons enabled the neural networks to learn any function. But those outside the field were discouraged from using the method. Funding began to favour the symbolic logic-based AI approaches.

AI would soon become dominated by symbolic logic. But even this miracle approach, which seemed so full of promise, had some issues. In 1969, McCarthy and British computer scientist Patrick Hayes pointed out that logic had some problems of its own. If you represent the world and behaviours within that world purely using logical statements, then every time something changes, you need to update everything relevant. But when some things may affect each other (moving a cup containing a spoon on to a table also moves the spoon), and some may not (the table may not be moved when the cup is placed on it), then you need more and more rules to accompany every new object and behaviour you represent. Such rules are known as frame axioms, which tell the computer what will not happen as well as what will happen. The frame problem is then how to make AI systems that could cope with real-world scenarios without becoming overwhelmed with the need for endless frame axioms. While the difficulty would eventually be overcome in logic after some years of effort, philosophers found the whole concept troubling. If an AI were one day to have near-human level intellect – and it was storing and updating its information about the world using this type of rigidly applied method – then its monumental database of facts and relationships between them would become intractable. It would be too slow and require too many rules to handle the real world.

Nevertheless, the die had been cast. While interest in the race to make AI seemed to be diminishing, the symbolic logic-based approaches were taking an early lead.

CHAPTER 010

1970-1980

First AI Winter

The Birth of the Computer Age

With the help of Ted Hoff (see previous chapter), the first commercial microprocessor was on sale in 1971. The Intel 4004, used primarily in Busicom desktop calculators, demonstrated the potential for large-scale integration of transistors on a chip and triggered the never-ending race by chip manufacturers to make faster, better, cheaper microprocessors. By the end of the decade, many foundational computer processor designs had been produced: the Intel 8080 as used in the MITS Altair 8800 kit that triggered a home computer boom, leading to copycats such as the Motorola 6800. This powerful processor powered high-end Unix workstations, and then generations of Mac computers, the Atari ST and Amiga computers, Sega game consoles and arcade machines. Its core is still found in embedded processors for car internal combustion engines and weather stations. The Z80 was an advanced clone of the 8800 and powered hundreds of business computers in the 1970s and was eventually used for the ZX Spectrum, Nintendo Game Boy, the Sega Master System and many graphing calculators. It was also the first in a long line of processors used in PCs in future years (the 8086, the 8088 and all the x86 chips). The 6502 was a cheaper rival to the 8088 and was used by Steve Wozniak in the first Apple II computers.

As computer technology increased, networking solutions were invented to connect them together. The beginnings of the Internet were created in the 1970s with the ARPANET and the fundamental Internet communication protocols being created. The familiar operating systems were also well under development: UNIX (which evolved in many directions including into Mac-OS), and PC-DOS (which became MS-DOS and subsequently Windows).

Truly the computer had arrived and was increasingly available for all.

Troubling Times for Artificial Intelligence

While computer technology boomed, artificial intelligence in the early 1970s did not. Compared to the miracles of the new microprocessors, advanced operating systems and networking, to some AI now looked dated and somehow lacking the rigour of 'real computer science'. Its failure to live up to the hype of the 1960s was becoming increasingly apparent.

The late 1960s saw problems highlighted in the US (see previous chapter). In 1972, the UK's main science funding body (the Science Research Council) commissioned a report on the progress of AI following severe disagreement in the field – often evident within Edinburgh University, which housed the premiere AI research centre for the UK at the time. Cambridge mathematician Sir James Lighthill wrote a report detailing his findings and followed it up with a televised debate, in which he (the 'accuser') debated the three AI experts Donald Michie and Richard Gregory (Department of Machine Intelligence,

Edinburgh University) and John McCarthy (Stanford) in a courtroom-like setting. He accused – with arms frequently flung out for effect – AI researchers of bad science because they oversimplified very complex problems. He suggested AI results so far were irrelevant because they had failed to achieve the promised results after twenty years of effort and millions in funding.

The AI researchers did their best to counter this public attack, but with little success. The aftermath was devastating for AI research in the UK. Funding was cancelled for all universities except for Edinburgh and Essex. Most AI funding simply dried up. While computer technology grew to become commonplace, AI research became a backwater of computer science. The period became known as the first AI Winter.

Other Kinds of Intelligence

While the AI researchers were reeling from the negative response to their work (and in many cases were looking for new jobs), research in other areas of computer science remained unaffected. One example was work by a computer scientist and engineer known as Lotfi Zadeh. Born in Azerbaijan, educated in Iran and then MIT and Columbia Universities in the USA, Zadeh eventually settled at the University of California, Berkeley, for most of his career, where he performed research into computer control systems. Although highly related to artificial intelligence, control systems had remained more in the realm of electrical engineering and so the field was shielded from the fallout of the AI Winter. After several years of research, Zadeh decided that there was a need for a new kind of control system. He appreciated the clarity of logic as used in some expert systems but felt that logic was inappropriate for accurate control with its binary on or off nature. For example, while you could control a lift (elevator) with logical on or off

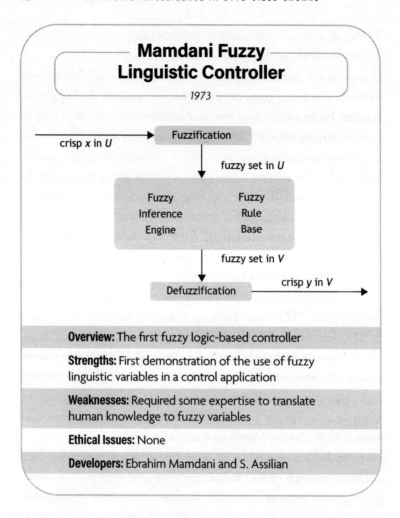

Mamdani Fuzzy Linguistic Controller

1973

crisp *x* in *U* → Fuzzification

fuzzy set in *U*

Fuzzy Inference Engine   Fuzzy Rule Base

fuzzy set in *V*

Defuzzification → crisp *y* in *V*

Overview: The first fuzzy logic-based controller

Strengths: First demonstration of the use of fuzzy linguistic variables in a control application

Weaknesses: Required some expertise to translate human knowledge to fuzzy variables

Ethical Issues: None

Developers: Ebrahim Mamdani and S. Assilian

instructions: go up / stop and go down / stop, this will result in a terrifying ride for passengers. The lift would jump to full speed instantly and stop instantly, throwing everyone off their feet. An appropriate controller for a lift must smoothly accelerate the lift from stationary to its top speed and then – even trickier – it must decelerate smoothly, coming to a halt at exactly the desired floor level: not a centimetre too high or too low.

Zadeh felt that logic needed to be *fuzzified* to account for this need for smoothness in control. Instead of having two logical values of true/false or on/off, he developed the idea that fuzzy logic could represent degrees of truth or shades of grey between one value and another. He first developed the idea in the mid-1960s, stating it in terms of membership of fuzzy sets, but it was not until the early 1970s that he developed it further for control, introducing ideas of linguistic variables to help encode human knowledge: a 'hot temperature' or 'wealthy customer'. The first real example of a fuzzy logic controller, which made use of linguistic variables, was created by researchers Ebrahim Mamdani and PhD student Sedrak Assilian at Queen Mary University of London. In 1973 they developed their fuzzy linguistic controller for a 'model industrial plant (a steam engine)' – used for a real cement plant in Denmark. It was published by doctoral student Assilian as his PhD thesis, explicitly calling it 'Artificial Intelligence in the Control of Real Dynamic Systems'. This new kind of AI made use of a knowledge base (a bit like an expert system) which included a fuzzy rule base, which when combined with some fuzzy mapping and signal processing formed a smart controller that made use of human knowledge and was capable of smooth control. It eventually became known as the Mamdani Controller.

Fuzzy logic took a while to be accepted, but it grew to become a major research field, becoming especially popular in Asia. It eventually became a standard method of 'smart control' lift controllers, rice cookers and ovens. To this day you'll find many such products still boast of their fuzzy controllers or fuzzy AI.

A Shakey Start

Controlling robots had always been one appealing application of AI. If you could make a computer brain that enabled a robot to navigate its world and behave appropriately then this surely would be intelligence in action. Shakey the robot was one pioneering example, developed from the late 1960s to the early 1970s at the Artificial Intelligence Center of the Stanford Research Institute. Shakey (so named because of its somewhat unsteady movements as it trundled around) was revolutionary at the time as it combined previously disconnected AI research in search, planning, natural language processing and vision. Computer scientists Charles Rosen, Nils Nilsson and Peter Hart led the project, which was funded by DARPA and developed in LISP.

Shakey was not a particularly fast or clever robot, and its brain was not carried with it – the computers were much too large and so needed to be connected via radio link. Shakey also existed only in an artificially created environment containing giant blocks such as cubes and pyramids as it was not very good at understanding what it was seeing – exactly the simplifications so abhorred by Lighthill in his report. But Shakey helped the researchers develop several important advances in AI. They created the idea of a *visibility graph* – where every point (*node*) is a location, which is connected (by an *edge*) if there is no obstacle between them. They invented the A* search algorithm – a much more efficient way of searching what to do and where to go next. They also advanced the nascent field of computer vision with the Hough Transform – a voting method to extract features from the camera image, detecting lines and eventually positions of shapes such as circles. More than a decade later, Shakey's successor, Flakey the Robot, would make use of fuzzy logic in its control systems. In a very real sense, Shakey was the grandfather of modern autonomous robots and self-driving vehicles.

Nilsson was to have a long and industrious career in AI at Stanford, also helping to invent the idea of automated planning in his 'Stanford Research Institute Problem Solver' (STRIPS), developed with his colleague Richard Fikes. STRIPS enabled the specification of clear goals given an initial state, and the set of

Shakey the Robot

1966–1972

Overview: Early autonomous robot

Strengths: Innovated several novel methods such as Hough Transform and A* algorithm

Weaknesses: Slow, and very limited in its ability to navigate; existed only in an artificially constructed room of large blocks

Ethical Issues: None

Developers: Charles Rosen, Nils Nilsson and Peter Hart and many others

actions. For example, your goal might be to place a cup on a table, given the initial state of holding the cup, and actions of moving to the table, and of moving your arm and hand. An action could have preconditions – for example, before you can place the cup on a table you need to have the table in front of you – and postconditions – once the cup is released on to the table, it is no longer in your hand.

STRIPS helped form the foundations of what became known as action languages, used by automated planners.

Evolving Intelligence

Researchers had already shown that search played an important part of AI, helped by algorithms such as A*. But some scientists took the idea even further. Just as neural networks were inspired by the human brain, genetic algorithms were inspired by the process of natural evolution. John Holland wrote a book on genetic algorithms in 1975 after several years of research into the use of evolution to help solve problems. His idea was simple: if natural evolution could optimize life so that offspring tended to have better fitness for their environments compared to their parents, then why could we not use the same principles in our computers to solve problems? His genetic algorithms maintained a population of candidate solutions to a given problem. Each solution would be a set of parameters that could be evaluated via a fitness function to determine how well they solved the problem. Those solutions that received a higher fitness score were selected preferentially as parents. Parent solutions would then generate a new population of child solutions that inherited genes from their parents. Holland created these digital genes by using binary coding: every parameter was stored as a binary number and then the resulting binary string of ones and zeros could be randomly mixed with sections taken from each parent to make a child, with a few random mutations thrown in for good measure. Starting with a population of random solutions, the genetic algorithm would then evolve better and better solutions to a problem.

It worked remarkably well, and Holland – who was a professor of multiple disciplines (psychology, electrical engineering and computer science) at the University of Michigan, Ann Arbor –

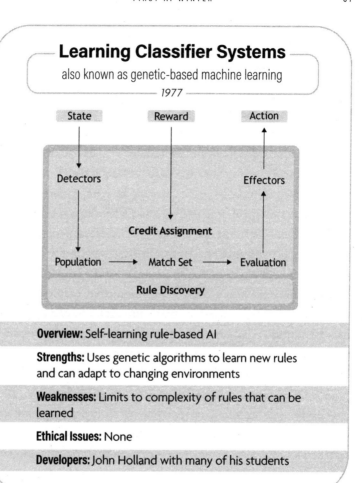

Learning Classifier Systems

also known as genetic-based machine learning

1977

State   Reward   Action

Detectors   Effectors

Credit Assignment

Population ⟶ Match Set ⟶ Evaluation

Rule Discovery

Overview: Self-learning rule-based AI

Strengths: Uses genetic algorithms to learn new rules and can adapt to changing environments

Weaknesses: Limits to complexity of rules that can be learned

Ethical Issues: None

Developers: John Holland with many of his students

soon expanded the idea to AI. In 1977, he began experiments with learning classifier systems. These were genetic algorithms that could learn new rules in response to a changing environment, where those rules could represent anything from controlling a robot to playing a game of draughts. A special 'bucket brigade' algorithm figured out which rules were responsible for the success or not of the classifier (rule) at a given point in time and assigned credit to the better ones, enabling them to have more children while worse rules were removed. In this way, learning classifier systems could teach themselves to perform new tasks. This was the start of something significant, and both genetic algorithms and learning classifier systems were to expand into major research fields that continue to this day.

Holland was not the only researcher to make use of evolution in computers in the 1970s, with several related algorithms being created that worked in a similar manner. Lawrence Fogel created one notable example. Fogel had some success in electrical engineering in the 1950s and 1960s, producing the first patents for noise-cancelling headphones – originally designed for helicopter pilots. In the 1960s, Fogel worked briefly for the National Science Foundation (NSF) and began an interest in cybernetics. He developed a theory that an artificial intelligence could be created using evolution on a computer, in contrast to the prevailing ideas of symbolic logic and expert systems. He proceeded to do his thesis on the topic and later wrote a book: *Artificial Intelligence Through Simulated Evolution.*

Fogel's idea was a combination of a simple evolutionary algorithm that only used mutation combined with Finite State Machines (invented a few years earlier by Edward Moore, a colleague of Claude Shannon). The FSM is a way of describing a system or machine which has behaviours and a predefined set of states. For example, a robot might have states 'move forward' and 'rotate left'. It would transition between those states depending on some sensory input, for example an obstacle encountered in front when in the 'move forward' state may make it switch to 'rotate left', which might switch back to 'move forward' again when the obstacle is no longer detected. Connect an evolutionary algorithm to the FSM and you can evolve the FSM – inventing and optimizing the states and transitions between them.

Evolutionary Programming
(of Finite State Machines)
1966

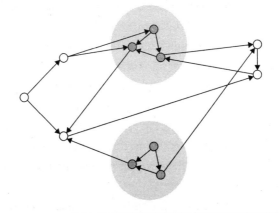

Overview: Self-learning finite state machine AI

Strengths: Uses a mutation-based evolutionary algorithm to learn new FSM states and transitions

Weaknesses: Limits to complexity of FSMs that can be learned, slow evaluation of fitness

Ethical Issues: None

Developer: Lawrence Fogel

Although Fogel was ahead of his time, first creating evolutionary programming in the 1960s before most other algorithms had been created, and refining it in the 1970s, his methods did not receive the same attention as Holland's genetic algorithms. Most evolution-based algorithms eventually became merged into the field of genetic algorithms, later known as evolutionary computation. Nevertheless, Fogel's son David spent much of his career continuing his father's work on evolutionary programming and making significant contributions himself.

Life, But Not as You Know It

Finite state machines as used in evolutionary programming are related to cellular automata, the method used by von Neumann in his exploration of universal constructors (see chapter 000). A cellular automata algorithm uses a grid where each cell can take one of a finite number of states, with the state transition determined by the state of the neighbouring cells, and the entire grid of cells being updated together to switch their states simultaneously. In 1970, Cambridge mathematician John Conway used this idea for something new.

Conway had started his studies as a 'terribly introverted adolescent' who liked to go around barefooted. By the end of a long career studying mathematics at Cambridge (and later at Princeton University, fittingly as the John von Neumann Chair of Mathematics), he was described as 'a cross between Archimedes, Mick Jagger and Salvador Dalí'. Back in 1970, Conway was obsessed with games as well as mathematics. Working only on paper, he invented a kind of cellular automata that behaved very strangely. So strangely, in fact, that it became known as Conway's Game of Life.

The rules of the game of life were very simple: cells could have one of two states: 'alive' or 'dead'. A live cell surrounded by fewer than two other live cells will die, as if by underpopulation. A live cell with two or three neighbours stays living. A live cell with more neighbours than that will die, as if by overpopulation. A dead cell with three live cells around it becomes a live cell, as if by reproduction.

Place a few random 'seed' cells in the grid and run the cellular

Conway's Game of Life

1970

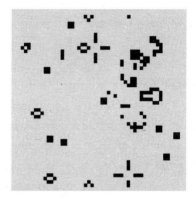

Overview: Most famous example of cellular automata

Strengths: Demonstrates complex lifelike behaviour with just a few simple rules

Weaknesses: Does not do anything useful beyond grow like bacteria

Ethical Issues: None

Developer: John Conway

automata, and something remarkable happens. There is a strange unpredictable growth, like bacteria spreading. Sometimes patterns form and move across the grid. Sometimes patterns stabilize and remain static. Sometimes patterns grow and then simply die off. It was remarkably lifelike.

Conway became something of a celebrity from this work, which was just one of many of his contributions in mathematics. He also kick-started the field of cellular automata, which was to develop into fascinating directions in the years to come. But his Game of Life was always his most famous invention, with thousands of 'Lifenthusiasts' spending hours programming their own patterns to enable special kinds of behaviours, from 'glider guns' to 'spaceships'.

Unusual Intelligence

Cellular automata (and evolutionary algorithms) were a typical example of a 'bottom up' approach to AI. Researchers start with the smallest components of life and try to grow intelligent behaviour incrementally. But the prevailing view of AI in the 1970s was still 'top down' – researchers would look at a desired intelligent behaviour and try to engineer a system to mimic that behaviour directly. Chatterbots were a prime example of this, and work on them did not stop despite the chill in the air for researchers.

ELIZA might have been a breakthrough in the 1960s, but by the 1970s researchers could do a bit better. Inspired by ELIZA and the AI work at Stanford, psychiatrist Kenneth Colby created a new chatterbot called PARRY in 1972. While ELIZA could play doctor, PARRY was designed to behave as a person with paranoid schizophrenia. As a Turing Test, in 1979 a panel of real psychiatrists were invited to communicate with real patients and PARRY through teleprinters. They were then asked to distinguish between real people and the AI. They guessed correctly only 48 per cent of the time – no different from random guessing.

PARRY was a more advanced chatterbot compared to ELIZA, mimicking emotional responses to certain triggers. This became very clear when the two were allowed to communicate over the ARPANET. Here's a fragment of their conversion:

ELIZA: Good Evening.

ELIZA: Tell me your problems. Please terminate input
       with a period or a question mark.
PARRY: People get on my nerves sometimes.
ELIZA: I am not sure I understand you fully.
PARRY: You should pay more attention.
ELIZA: Suppose you should pay more attention.
PARRY: You're entitled to your own opinion.
ELIZA: What makes you think I am entitled to my own
       opinion?
PARRY: It bothers me just to be around people in
       general.
ELIZA: Please go on.
PARRY: I went to the track at Bay Meadows a while
       back.
ELIZA: What does that suggest to you?
PARRY: I went to the races.
ELIZA: What else would you like to discuss?
PARRY: Horse racing interests me.
ELIZA: Why do you say that just now?
PARRY: There's a lot of crooked gambling going on
       there.
ELIZA: I am not sure I understand you fully.
PARRY: It's clear to me if not to you.
ELIZA: Do you think it's likely that not to I?
PARRY: I went to the races.
ELIZA: Please go on.
PARRY: I gamble on horses.
ELIZA: What does that suggest to you?
PARRY: I went to the races.
ELIZA: What else would you like to discuss?
PARRY: Gambling has been nothing but trouble to me.
ELIZA: Why do you say that just now?
PARRY: I've had experience with crooks gambling at
       the track.
ELIZA: I am not sure I understand you fully.

And so on...

PARRY

1972

Overview: Chatterbot with paranoid schizophrenia

Strengths: More advanced chatterbot able to fool experts

Weaknesses: Only able to communicate in a very specific way, mimicking a patient with paranoid schizophrenia

Ethical Issues: Is it appropriate for an AI to mimic human mental illness?

Developer: Kenneth Colby

PARRY was not the only AI to progress natural language processing. SHRDLU (named after the set of keys next to each other on a Linotype machine keyboard) was developed by Terry Winograd at MIT for his PhD. This simple AI operated in a simplified 'blocks world' and could understand and respond to queries about the world, for example: 'Is the red sphere on top of the green cube?'

The blocks world was again exactly the kind of simplification so vilified by Lighthill in his report a couple of years later. Surprisingly, Lighthill's pessimism was reinforced by the creator of ELIZA. In 1976, Weizenbaum wrote a book *Computer Power and Human Reason*. He argued that computers and AI should never be permitted to make important decisions for they will always lack wisdom and compassion. He distinguished between making a decision – something a computer can do based on logical rules – and making a choice – something that requires judgement. His arguments were to alienate him from many AI researchers at the time, and only helped deepen the AI Winter.

Researchers like Terry Winograd were discouraged but did not give up. Winograd moved to Stanford and continued his research into AI for understanding natural language for many years. He also supervised two notable PhD students: Sergey Brin and Larry Page. Brin later recalled that Winograd had encouraged him to pursue his idea of understanding the World Wide Web as a network of graphs, saying, 'It was the best advice I ever received.' After some research, Brin and Page founded a company called Google in 1998.

Audible Intelligence

Understanding natural language in the form of written sentences was one thing, but most everyday human communication is through the spoken word. An AI that could understand our speech would be hugely useful. These were the thoughts of Raj Reddy, an Indian-born computer scientist who had finished his PhD at John McCarthy's AI Lab at Stanford and was moving to Carnegie Mellon University. Reddy founded speech-recognition work at CMU, and eventually created several departments (and supported several other universities) in the effort to enable computers understand human speech.

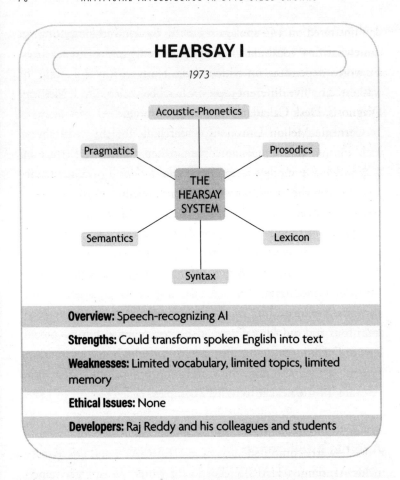

HEARSAY I

1973

Acoustic-Phonetics

Pragmatics

Prosodics

THE HEARSAY SYSTEM

Semantics

Lexicon

Syntax

Overview: Speech-recognizing AI

Strengths: Could transform spoken English into text

Weaknesses: Limited vocabulary, limited topics, limited memory

Ethical Issues: None

Developers: Raj Reddy and his colleagues and students

Hearsay 1 was their first speech-understanding AI. It processed audio to derive sound characteristics (phonetics), stress and intonation patterns, a dictionary of words, a set of language grammar rules, meanings of words and sentences and context of the conversation to resolve ambiguities. While limited in its vocabulary, and a little slow because of the processing ability of the computers at the time, Hearsay 1 was a remarkable achievement and could process simple sentences turning audio into text correctly 89 per cent of the time. By October 1973, it had been demonstrated on 144 spoken sentences by five speakers. It had a somewhat tiny vocabulary of between twenty-eight and seventy-six words depending on which topic it was set up to handle. It was tested on five different topics: Chess, News Retrieval, Medical Diagnosis, Desk Calculator and Programming.

Carnegie Mellon University research flourished in the area, with another researcher named Jim Baker suggesting the use of *hidden Markov* models (a mathematical model of a sequence of events where the probability of an event depends on the previous event) to process the audio. Jim called his system DRAGON. Its mathematical foundation meant that it calculated probabilities of words and how likely they were to occur next to each other – rather like how an autocorrect system works today on a phone. When described in 1975 it was unclear how well it worked as it had been tested on just nine sentences. Nevertheless, Baker was ambitious and quickly released it as a commercial product called DragonDictate. By 1982, he and his wife had created Dragon Systems, a company that continued to release audio-recognition software for the next forty years and is still going today.

Meanwhile, Reddy and his group continued their work, developing several more speech-recognition AIs. PhD student Bruce Lowerre combined ideas from HEARSAY 1 and DRAGON in his AI, named HARPY. As more talented researchers joined Reddy's lab, so the speech-recognizing AIs improved further. HEARSAY II built on the advances of the previous systems and added a 'blackboard' system – a virtual place where the separate software agents could share their findings with each other, improving communication between them and enabling them to collaborate on the same problem. This idea was to be inherited by many AIs in future years.

You've Been Framed

With so many attempts at developing AIs to represent knowledge about the world, in MIT, Minsky realized that it was necessary to have some coherent way to store this information. Expanding on the neat ideas of logic favoured by his colleagues in Stanford, Minsky created a slightly more 'scruffy' approach, that he named the frame. This was a novel data structure – a table of information about objects, for example the object 'Boy' might have 'slots' such as 'ISA: Person' (a pointer to a parent frame Person), 'Gender: Male', 'Residence: Address' (where address is another frame) and so on. Slots could also take 'procedural attachments' – code to give them further flexibility. Frames were highly related to object-oriented languages and the semantic web, to come later. From his 1974 work, frames soon evolved into languages such as KRL (Knowledge Representation Language) developed by Bobrow and Winograd, and later KL-ONE. Eventually they helped the development of ontologies such as the Web Ontology Language (OWL) that became a standard for representing knowledge on the Internet.

As Minsky continued to work on AI, he also began developing his own theory of how brains worked. Through much of the 1970s, working with colleague Seymour Papert, he began to describe his view of intelligence. 'Minds are what brains do,' he believed, describing our intelligence as something that arises from the interactions of many diverse agents, each of which may store and process information differently for different purposes. He called this idea 'the society of minds' and contrasted it with the alternative view of AI at the time that there must be some fundamental principle or single formal system behind intelligence.

The widening gap between those who preferred formal, logical methods of AI and those who did not, helped separate researchers into what became known as the 'neats' and the 'scruffies'.

Learning to Think

Mainstream AI (or what remained of the field) was dominated by symbolic processing in the 1970s. In addition to LISP, another language known as Prolog had been created in 1972 from the Universities of Edinburgh and Aix-Marseille, further cementing this idea in AI.

But not all researchers were interested in this approach, and work on neural networks continued. Paul Werbos had started his interest in computers and the brain while a student working as an intern for a doctor in the 1960s. He had been shown Hebb's book and found it fascinating, but realized a neural network on a computer needed a method to learn the values of the weights. 'Hebbian learning' (see chapter 000) wouldn't do it. Once at Harvard, he took a neuroscience course and did his best to understand how brains might learn, thinking of ideas such as reinforcement learning. Then one day he shared a car with some people and chatted about his problem – how to optimize the weights of a neural network automatically. One of them told him about dynamic programming. This was what he needed to combine various ideas and create a neural network that learned using *backpropagation*, using reinforcement learning. He published his groundbreaking PhD thesis on backpropagation in neural networks in 1974.

While the separate ideas were old and well-established concepts in mathematics, backpropagation was nevertheless a breakthrough as the method permits multi-layer perceptrons to be trained in an efficient and fast manner. Returning to our metaphor of the first chapter, our neuron is like a major road tunnel under a river, multiple roads converging on the entrance each with their own speed limits, and a traffic light on the output of the tunnel. Change the speed limits (neuron weights) and depending on the amount of traffic on each input road, the traffic light will be green or red (the neuron will be activated or not).

When we train the neuron, we need to change the weights so that it activates only for certain values on certain inputs. One could imagine we have a convoy of VIP vehicles coming on only some of the input roads and we have to set the speed limits such that the traffic light is green for them, and they get through. (We have a pattern of values on the inputs and we want the neuron to respond correctly at the output.) When training, we make many attempts and see how successful we were each time. If the VIP convoy makes it through then the neuron worked correctly that time. But if not, then we have an error. We know what we wanted and we know what we actually got; the difference is the error value (it's often a good idea to square this value so that bigger errors are magnified more). We can then go back and update the speed limits proportionately according to their values. (A larger value that let a lot of traffic through may be more to blame for the error compared to a low value that had little effect on the output.) We update the values a few times up or down until we minimize the error seen at the output, using a learning rule (today often an optimization method such as gradient descent, see chapter 100). If our traffic light has a complicated non-linear transformation function (which later neural networks use as they enable learning of more complex data), then we have to use a bit of calculus and take the derivative of the function when figuring out the error.

The clever bit about backpropagation is that we can keep following the same procedure even when we connect neurons together into layers (our tunnel output joins to a road that goes to another tunnel with another traffic light, which feeds to another road that goes to another tunnel, and so on). We can use some clever maths to propagate the error backwards, figuring out all the derivatives as we go. Then as we optimize weights according to our learning rule, we can figure out the new error at the output, and then propagate that error back, try new weight values, and so on.

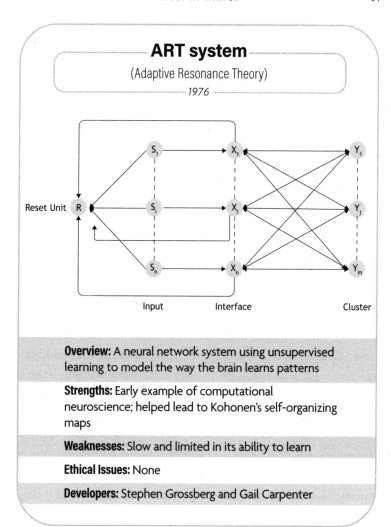

ART system
(Adaptive Resonance Theory)
1976

Reset Unit

Input   Interface   Cluster

Overview: A neural network system using unsupervised learning to model the way the brain learns patterns

Strengths: Early example of computational neuroscience; helped lead to Kohonen's self-organizing maps

Weaknesses: Slow and limited in its ability to learn

Ethical Issues: None

Developers: Stephen Grossberg and Gail Carpenter

Werbos spent his career making advances in neural networks. For a time he was programme director of the National Science Foundation, using his position to help fund projects that progressed research in the area. But in the 1970s, Werbos was too early. His work did not receive the attention it deserved for more than a decade – indeed Werbos said of this work in 2023, 'When I first proposed backpropagation, nobody would believe my claims. I had so many arguments with so many people who said, "This is crazy." It took decades to persuade them.'

Werbos was not the only scientist working in this area at the time. In 1975, Stephen Grossberg was already a full professor at Boston University, having made substantial discoveries in the use of computers to understand the brain and perform theoretical neuroscience, which became known as computational neuroscience. In 1976, working with colleague Gail Carpenter, he developed a series of neural network AIs that he called ART (Adaptive Resonance Theory). Intended to model the way the brain worked, their neurons learned patterns in an unsupervised manner. Instead of being explicitly trained according to how well they produced a desired output as with supervised learning, ART systems updated their neurons based on how well each neuron's weights matched an input vector, with neurons naturally converging to represent different parts of a dataset. Multiple ART AIs were developed over the years, including Fuzzy ART systems that used fuzzy logic. By 1980, similar ideas were used by Finnish computer scientist Teuvo Kohonen in his method, called the *self-organizing map*.

As the 1970s came to a close, the criticisms of AI were now becoming a memory. There were new and better computers available. New researchers were emerging who were motivated not just by trying to mimic intelligent behaviour, but also by trying to understand the inner workings of the brain. AI was coming back.

CHAPTER 011

1980-1990

The Birth of New Intelligence

Take On Me

With microcomputers and electronic devices now being mass-produced, the first synthesizers for music became popular in the 1980s, heralding a period of synth-pop classics (as well as a lot of denim). Walkmans and boomboxes became widespread, bringing music closer to people. The first VCRs became established, with VHS winning the format race over Betamax. The compact disc was also invented for the audiophiles, spelling the beginning of the end for vinyl – at least for the next thirty years or so.

While the 1970s saw the first business computers, the 1980s brought a home computer boom with ordinary families now able to purchase computers and game consoles. The Internet became a reality from the mid-1980s, and the beginnings of the World Wide Web started by the end of the decade in CERN. For the first time, computers began to be used in the movie industry for special effects: a morphing spaceship in *Flight of the Navigator*, water effects in *The Abyss*, and a whole movie set inside a computer in *Tron*.

The population was increasingly tech-savvy and eager for the latest gadgets. It was the perfect environment for a new wave of AI methods to emerge into.

Chinese Rooms

But the road has never been smooth for AI researchers. American philosopher John Searle had always been a somewhat contrary thinker at University of California, Berkeley where he was a professor, joining the Free Speech Movement in the 1960s and challenging rent control rules by Berkeley in the 1980s.

In 1980, Searle wrote a groundbreaking critique of current AI systems as he saw them. Searle disliked the claims of 'Strong AI', which seemed to be saying that if a computer could behave as though it had a mind, then it had one. If it looks like a duck and quacks like a duck, then it's a duck. He created a thought experiment to prove this idea was flawed.

Searle imagined an AI inside a room that could behave as though it understood the Chinese language perfectly. Feed it Chinese characters on paper through a slot and it would output Chinese responses on new pieces of paper. The AI could converse perfectly in Chinese using this method, and appeared as natural as any human in its conversation, easily passing the Turing Test. Searle then asked: does this AI actually understand Chinese (Strong AI), or is it merely simulating an ability to converse in Chinese (Weak AI)?

Searle then imagined himself inside a room. He would take pieces of paper through a slot in the door, look up the symbols he saw in a filing cabinet and follow a set of instructions on which symbols to push out again. He was effectively following the AI's program by hand. At no point does he understand what any of the symbols mean. He is just following rules. Searle suggested that there was no difference to the way he was behaving in his Chinese

Room compared to the AI. So if he did not understand Chinese, then the AI could not either. It must be that the AI was simulating the ability to converse in Chinese – weak AI. It might look like a duck and quack like a duck, but underneath it is not a duck at all.

For the simple AIs that operated using symbolic processing, Searle's argument was cogent. These AIs did simply shuffle symbols around and had no understanding of how those symbols or the rules they followed corresponded to anything in our physical world. But cognitive scientists spent many decades making counter-arguments to prove Searle wrong. For example, replace Searle inside his Chinese Room with a human brain of a Chinese speaker and look deeply at the individual neurons. Does any single neuron understand Chinese? Yet working together they can have that understanding. If a computer built up its knowledge and behaviour using programs that worked in that way, why would it not understand Chinese as deeply as a human brain?

Thinking with Neurons

In 1982, the chilly winter of AI came to an end at last, prompted partly by a new kind of neural network. Like many of the advances to come in the field of neural networks, the inventor of the method was often a little ahead of their time and didn't receive the recognition they deserved. In this case, Japanese pioneer Shun'ichi Amari (see chapter 001) created a type of neural network that behaved as a memory back in 1972. But it was not until John Hopfield created his version in 1982 that the field noticed.

John Hopfield was a multidisciplinary American scientist, whose career spanned physics, chemistry and biology. He was interested in the way the working of the brain might resemble networks seen in physics. Already the idea of an Ising model (named after physicist Ernst Ising) was well established: a mathematical model used in physics to explain *phase transitions* (a dramatic change of state). For example, a newly created ferrous metal might start in a state where many different parts of it are magnetized in opposite polarities. But each tiny element (magnetic dipole) will affect each other until they all tend to line up, agreeing on the same polarity. The Ising

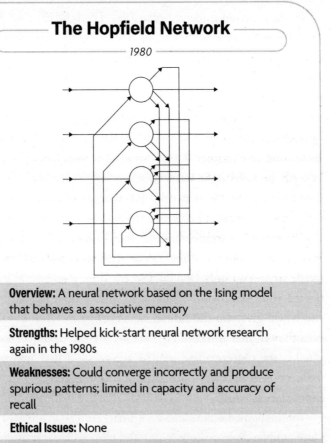

The Hopfield Network

1980

Overview: A neural network based on the Ising model that behaves as associative memory

Strengths: Helped kick-start neural network research again in the 1980s

Weaknesses: Could converge incorrectly and produce spurious patterns; limited in capacity and accuracy of recall

Ethical Issues: None

Developers: John Hopfield (original concept by Shun'ichi Amari)

model is a mathematical model that mimics this process. It uses a grid of cells rather like cellular automata, where each element of the grid could represent one or the other state. Each element is allowed to interact with its neighbours with the result that they all tend to relax into a state where they agree with each other. Hopfield wondered if this same idea could apply to the brain, particularly in relation to memory.

He constructed a neural network based on the Ising model. Just one layer of fully connected neurons was used (meaning the output of every neuron is connected to the input of every neuron, in a recurrent network). Each neuron is either firing or not firing, and the list (vector) of one or zero neuron states for any given input represents the state for the overall network. The network is trained by updating the weights of the neurons according to Hebb's law of association (see chapter 000). The weights then force the neurons to settle into the right states to represent the desired output, for a given input to the network. The weights of every connection represent information being stored.

The result is a strange kind of neural network that acts like an associative memory. It's like you remembering the full name of a movie when you only hear part of the title: *Back to the* … Once trained you can provide the network with a vague or partial input and it will give you the full answer: *Back to the Future*. Hopfield even showed that you could get the network to optimize problems – tell it the objective and any constraints and its neurons could settle themselves into a state where the objective was met and constraints satisfied.

The network became known (perhaps a little unfairly) as the Hopfield Network.

Reinforced Thinking

Neural network research continued to expand with another foundational AI created the following year in 1983. Andrew Barto was an American computer scientist based at the University of Massachusetts. Following a PhD on cellular automata, Barto developed an interest in neural networks, and together with his first PhD students Richard Sutton and Chuck Anderson, developed a new kind of neural network architecture which built on work by others such as Widrow (see chapter 001).

Barto was interested in unsupervised learning, specifically the idea of reinforcement learning – the neural network should get feedback from trying out its behaviour and if that behaviour seemed to be improving then it should do more of the same; if its behaviour was becoming worse it should not do that any further. They imagined a task of a cart with a pole on the top of it. The cart could move left or right, and its movements would attempt to balance the pole. Move left rapidly and the pole would topple to the right. But if the pole starts to topple right then moving right might correct its motion and keep it balanced upright. It's an ideal kind of problem for reinforcement learning as it can provide constant feedback on how well the neural network is doing as it moves the cart.

Barto knew that conventional neural networks struggled a little with this problem. Inspired by ideas of learning in animals, he created a kind of two-in-one neural network, composed of an *actor* and a *critic*. The actor neural network (associative search element, or ASE) would behave as normal, receiving input from its environment (the current state of the cart and pole) and acting to move the cart to try and balance the pole. He made the problem more difficult by providing only limited feedback: an error when the pole was about to fall over, or the cart had reached the end of its track. He then added the critic (adaptive critic element,

Actor-Critic Reinforcement Learning

1983

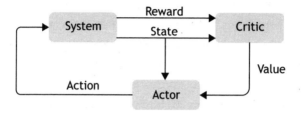

Overview: Uses an 'adaptive critic element' to help the 'associative search element' neural network in a pole-balancing task

Strengths: Laid the foundations for actor-critic RL

Weaknesses: Very simple 'neural networks' – not much more than single neuron-like elements

Ethical Issues: None

Developers: Andrew Barto, Richard Sutton and Charles Anderson

or ACE): a neural network that learned to fill in the missing information and figure out how well the actor was doing. The result was surprisingly good – the collaboration between the two neural networks resulted in much better control compared to a previous attempt by other researchers.

Actor-critic reinforcement learning was launched from this promising start and its inventors continued working in the field for the rest of their careers. Eventually, more than thirty years later, in 2016 a new way of training actor-critic networks would be invented, known as Asynchronous Advantage Actor-Critic (A3C), with the result that progress in this form of reinforcement learning would leap forward.

But the 1980s were a good decade for reinforcement learning in general. British computer scientist Chris Watkins spent his graduate years studying how children learned, setting them tasks and trying to understand how they would learn to improve. He was inspired by the actor-critic model of Sutton and Barto, and he was aware that behavioural ecologists were modelling animal behaviour using dynamic programming. So for his PhD he developed his own form of reinforcement learning that made use of dynamic programming. It became known as Q-learning.

Watkins used the idea of a Markov Decision Process (MDP) – it's a bit like the finite state machine (see chapter 010), only instead of representing a system as a set of finite states with deterministic transitions between them, the MDP switches between states based on probabilities. If the probability of switching state is always 1, then the MDP acts just like an FSM. But most of the time, the MDP uses different probabilities. An AI that uses an MDP must figure out what action to take for each state that it is in. This is known as finding the right policy. Since there's always a lot of maths involved, it means finding the right policy function to map from states to actions.

Watkins took this idea and ran with it, suggesting that you could use a new set of values known as Q values to figure out how good an action might be from a state. These values are calculated by looking at the 'temporal difference' between the value of the current state and action and the previous ones. The AI uses trial and error learning to figure out what to do, while building a 'Q table' of Q values to store past results (borrowing tricks from dynamic programming). It did its learning without even worrying

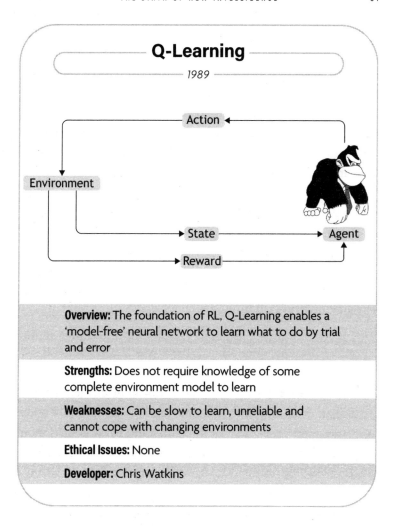

Q-Learning

1989

Overview: The foundation of RL, Q-Learning enables a 'model-free' neural network to learn what to do by trial and error

Strengths: Does not require knowledge of some complete environment model to learn

Weaknesses: Can be slow to learn, unreliable and cannot cope with changing environments

Ethical Issues: None

Developer: Chris Watkins

about policies for that pesky MDP. It did not need to worry about transition probabilities or expected rewards for the MDP at all. The result was an AI that figured out what to do by trial and error – learning what works when, and what does not, just as we do, without having an explicit model of the world.

Of course, Q-learning was not perfect. It effectively strings a series of guesses together, and if your earlier guesses about which action to take were flawed, you may not find out for a while – meaning it takes a long time to learn from the mistake, especially if you're trying to use Q-learning for practical applications such as robot control. Being 'off policy', it's not explicitly trying to find that optimal MDP policy – so it can sometimes end up with completely wrong solutions. And if the environment is changing (what was a good action to take five minutes ago is no longer a good action now), then Q-learning simply can't cope. While later researchers added a massive amount of computation and new deep learning algorithms to try and help, most of these fundamental problems never really went away.

Propagating Backwards

Paul Werbos may have published his work on backpropagation for training neural networks in 1974 (see chapter 010), but it was not until twelve years later that an experimental analysis was published in the influential journal *Nature* by psychologist David Rumelhart and computer scientists Geoff Hinton and Ronald Williams. The paper described the method as a 'new learning procedure' and while they cited Minsky and Rosenblatt's work, Werbos was not credited – an oversight that British scientist Hinton later tried to correct, saying, 'Lots of different people invented different versions of backpropagation before David Rumelhart. They were mainly independent inventions, and it's something I feel I have got too much credit for. I've seen things in the press that say that I invented backpropagation, and that is completely wrong. It's one of these rare cases where an academic feels he has got too much credit for something!'

Original inventors or not, their 1986 paper in *Nature* was widely reported and caused a huge stir in the field of neural network research. Suddenly AI was back, and it was being powered by neurons.

By 1989, researchers had progressed so far that the first practical application of multi-layer neural networks were emerging. French computer scientist Yann LeCun had completed his PhD by 1987 (during his research he also independently invented the back propagation algorithm – and was cited by the Rumelhart paper). He joined AT&T Bell Laboratories in New Jersey, USA where he developed systems to read handwriting – a tricky task, given the huge diversity of handwriting and writing instruments that people write with. LeCun and his colleagues decided a new kind of neural network was needed that operated in a similar way to the visual cortex in our brains. He called his neural network LeNet.

LeNet used backpropagation to learn the weights of a rather different kind of net. Now known as a convolutional neural network (CNN), it works by focusing on a tiny area of the image (just a 3x3 or 5x5 pixel square) with its receptive field and sweeping this little window (or *feature detector*) left to right, top to bottom until the whole image has been 'viewed' (a *convolution* has occurred). Each time the feature detector 'looks' at a new little segment of the image, it will combine what it sees into a summary value, or *convolved feature*. Use multiple feature detectors and you may find more things in the image – perhaps one for red, one for green and one for blue values. Perform another convolution (take the output summary values and treat them like a lower resolution version of the original image and apply more feature detectors) and you may help the network learn that tiny features are combined to make bigger features. An image of a bus is made from lines which together make shapes, which make wheels, windows and bodywork, which together make the bus.

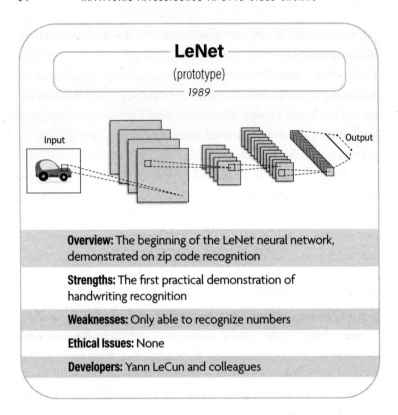

LeNet

(prototype)

1989

Input

Output

Overview: The beginning of the LeNet neural network, demonstrated on zip code recognition

Strengths: The first practical demonstration of handwriting recognition

Weaknesses: Only able to recognize numbers

Ethical Issues: None

Developers: Yann LeCun and colleagues

Once you've finished convolving the image, the result is then fed through an activation function to add some essential nonlinearity that makes neural networks powerful, then through pooling layers which downsample the image further, taking the maximum value of those produced by the receptive fields (max pooling) or the average of the values (average pooling) to reduce the amount of information further. Push all these values through a bunch of hidden layers (multiple layers of fully connected neurons) and then finally connect the output of the last layer to your output layer, which will be the set of neurons that 'talk' directly to you.

Although it's a complicated architecture (arrangement of neurons), underneath all the complexity were familiar multi-layer perceptrons, and so LeCun was able to use backpropagation to train his fancy neural network. It took three days – which was considered pretty good – and the result was that it could indeed read human handwriting. Or at least, handwritten zip code numbers provided by the US Postal Service. After rejecting 12 per cent of digits that it couldn't make sense of, it achieved 99 per cent accuracy. Once trained it was able to classify around ten digits per second.

A few years later and LeCun 5 was a full-blown 7-level CNN, which successfully performed optical character recognition for bank cheques (a solution that was widely used for the next decade in the banking industry).

AI is Back in Business

The 1980s were shaping up to be a good decade for AI. In addition to the advances with neural networks, other key advances were made. Simulated annealing had been introduced in 1980 – a search method a little like the genetic algorithm that finds good solutions to difficult problems – this time based on the way metal is annealed. (Like jiggling metal molecules, candidate solutions are randomly 'jiggled' by decreasing amounts until an optimum is found.) In 1986, Chris Langton, PhD student of John Holland, began a new kind of AI which he termed artificial life. He used cellular automata (not unlike John Conway) to study complex systems and suggested that living systems existed on a knife edge between order and disorder: on the edge of chaos. ALife soon became a research field in its own right, where researchers use computers to ask 'what if' questions about life: what if the first self-replicating molecules were different? What if evolution in a computer can help explain the evolution of natural organisms? It attracted researchers from disciplines as diverse as chemistry to philosophy and continues to this day.

ChipTest

(later known as Deep Thought and Deep Blue)

1985–1997

Overview: Optimized hardware to enable searching of half a million chess moves a second; later upgraded to be even faster

Strengths: The first AI to beat a chess grand master (eventually)

Weaknesses: Brute-force approach to game-playing

Ethical Issues: None

Developers: Feng-hsiung Hsu, Thomas Anantharaman, Murray Campbell, Arthur Joseph Hoane

But mainstream AI was still symbolic processing, and primarily expert systems. Many of the expert systems that began life in the 1960s had been quietly developed for twenty years and were considered mature and highly successful AI systems. Business now considered expert systems to be the technology of the moment, and two-thirds of Fortune 500 companies jumped on the bandwagon – making use of expert systems in their businesses.

IBM was one of those companies. Having transitioned from data tabulating machines to computer technology in the 1950s and 1960s, IBM had established themselves as a leader in business computing solutions. They wanted to keep expanding their reputation, and they heard of a research programme at Carnegie Mellon University where a team of computer scientists had built new chips that enabled a computer to search through chess moves faster than ever before. The researchers had called their AI 'ChipTest'. By 1987, a debugged version called ChipTest-M won the North American Computer Chess Championship. The team continued and a big brother to ChipTest was built, called Deep Thought (named after the fictional AI in *The Hitchhiker's Guide to the Galaxy*). In 1989, it won the World Computer Chess Championship and so they pitted Deep Thought against grand master Garry Kasparov. It lost 2-0. After completing their PhDs, the team were persuaded to join IBM with the aim of defeating a world chess champion. It was not to happen until 1997, with its new 'IBM' name of Deep Blue.

ChipTest and its successors were dedicated chess-playing AIs. They used an expert-system-like 'opening book' containing vast numbers of examples of good opening games (the first few moves of chess games) so that they would not fall into easy traps when the number of pieces on the board was still high and the possible number of moves was still astronomical. Once that was exhausted, they used pure brute search to look through the possible moves one by one to find the right move (using the minimax algorithm, see chapter 000). The final version was able to look from six to twenty moves ahead, considering billions of alternatives.

Expert Boom

Japan was not to be left behind in the new race for tech excellence. They also appreciated the idea that custom computer hardware might be the solution to make AI faster and even more profitable. So in 1982, the Ministry of International Trade and Industry announced that they would invest in the development of massively parallel computers to run logic-based languages such as Prolog. A new 'institute for new generation computer technology' was created which worked with eight computer manufacturers in Japan and many of the major Japanese research institutes. The Fifth Generation Computer Systems project ran for the next twelve years, with an investment of around 57 billion yen (about £310 million). A series of AIs were created, called Parallel Inference Machines (PIMs). The five custom machines (PIM/m, PIM/p, PIM/i, PIM/k, PIM/c) were optimized to run logic programming languages and expert systems (applications such as *Kappa*, a parallel database management system and *MGTP*, an automated theorem prover).

Not wanting to be left behind, the United States announced their own strategic computing initiative in 1983, which was to run for a decade. The aim of this billion-dollar funding exercise was to create 'full machine intelligence' by giving computers the ability 'to see, hear, speak and think like a human'. Hundreds of projects in academia and industry were funded, including the first efforts to create autonomous vehicles.

Meanwhile, the teams involved with successful expert systems had created startups to commercialize the underlying AI technologies. Teknowledge Inc stripped out the medical diagnosis rules of MYCIN and licensed the empty expert system as E-MYCIN. IntelliGenetics attempted to commercialize MOLGEN, later also licensing their expert system shell and renaming themselves IntelliCorp. The Carnegie Group attempted to generalize XCON. And the list of startups in the 1980s kept growing: Neuron Data made Nexpert, an expert system that ran on the Macintosh; AION made its own expert system of the same name; there was even a company with the unfortunate name of AIDS (AI decision systems).

With so much investment piling into the new expert system companies, and Japan investing heavily into its PIMs which would run expert systems faster and better, there also seemed to be an opportunity for companies to make money by supporting the anticipated new industry with custom hardware. A slew of companies were created to run LISP faster. The most well known of these derived from the work by Richard Greenblatt at MIT in the 1970s where he first developed new hard-wired computer architectures to speed up LISP language processing. The work became known as the MIT LISP Machine Project, and led to an MIT spin-off company Symbolics, Inc (the same company that briefly sold MACSYMA) which released its dedicated LISP machine, the LM-2, in 1981, followed by a series of very successful LISP machines throughout much of the 1980s (the 3600 series LISP machines).

This was not the only successful hardware company. Danny Hillis, a student of Marvin Minsky and Claude Shannon at MIT, had some ambitious ideas about the creation of a massively parallel computer architecture. He called it the Connection Machine, and not only did his PhD on the topic win the 1985 ACM (Association for Computing Machinery) dissertation award, he founded a company called Thinking Machines Corporation, recruiting numerous stellar minds (including Richard Feynman). Hillis and his team went on to build some of the fastest computers in the world, pioneering many ideas of parallel computing still in use today, with a focus on LISP and AI applications. Their first commercial release was the CM-1, followed by CM-2, CM-200, and the CM-5. The computers became widely used in the 1980s and perhaps because of their futuristic appearance were even featured in movies – in *Jurassic Park*, the dinosaur cloning video mentions the use of Thinking Machines supercomputers, and eight are visible in the park's control room.

A Second Chill

With so much enthusiasm and hundreds of millions being invested, mainstream artificial intelligence was a winner again. But the new-found popularity quickly started alarming those who were still warming their hands after the frostbite of the 1970s AI Winter. As early as 1984, with the last winter barely over, AI researchers were pondering whether the current feeding frenzy on expert systems would last. A debate held at the 1984 conference AAAI showed some fascinating insights at the time. The introduction by Yale computer scientist Drew McDermott almost said it all:

> In spite of all the commercial hustle and bustle around AI these days, there's a mood that I'm sure many of you are familiar with of deep unease among AI researchers who have been around more than the last four years or so. This unease is due to the worry that perhaps expectations about AI are too high, and that this will eventually result in disaster.
>
> To sketch a worst-case scenario, suppose that five years from now the strategic computing initiative collapses miserably as autonomous vehicles fail to roll. The fifth generation turns out not to go anywhere, and the Japanese government immediately gets out of computing. Every start-up company fails....
>
> I don't think this scenario is very likely to happen, nor even a milder version of it. But there is nervousness, and I think it is important that we take steps to make sure the 'AI Winter' doesn't happen – by disciplining ourselves and educating the public.

Roger Schank, director of the new Yale Artificial Intelligence Project, recounted some recent conversations at the same debate:

I was having a conversation with Oliver Selfridge, telling him about my new educational software company. I said, 'Well, it really doesn't have anything to do with AI at all, except that some of the software we design has to do with things like teaching, reading and reasoning comes from ideas that we've had in AI, but there's no AI in the programs in any way.' And he said, 'Oh, sort of like expert systems, huh?'

...The second conversation I had was with a real estate developer, who had a PhD in Biology. He wanted to build an expert systems industrial park; every company in it would be doing expert systems. I said, 'You may have come to the wrong person; I don't much believe in expert systems.' 'How can you say that?' he replied. 'To get computers to model everything that somebody knows; to put all the knowledge in and have the thing be just like a person – that's terrific.' I replied, 'Yes. But we don't know how to do that yet.' He said, 'No, but that's what expert systems are.'

And that was exactly the problem.

Failed Assumptions

It was still the 1980s. There was no World Wide Web containing the world's knowledge to mine. Most useful information was still stored on paper or within the minds of human experts. There were no readily available data at all for expert systems. Those few expert systems that had proven their worth had taken two decades of work to fill with information, laboriously entered by teams of domain and computer experts. Even when they were supplied with information about a topic, they still couldn't always reason about it properly and might return incorrect responses. It didn't really matter if you bought an 'empty expert system' for your business. It didn't matter if it was running on optimized hardware. How much time and manpower would it cost you to enter the information about your business – if you could retrieve and codify it properly at all? And if you went to the expense of creating thousands of rules within your expert system, how much time and cost does it take to maintain the rule base?

There were also fundamental questions being asked about the entire concept of symbolic AI. In 1988, a series of retrospective articles were written to summarize progress so far. In one, philosopher and computer scientist Hilary Putnam wrote, 'Currently the most touted achievement of AI is "expert systems". But these systems (which are, at bottom, just high-speed data-base searchers) are not models for any interesting mental capacities.' In another, Hubert Dreyfus (philosopher and long-time critic of AI) wrote, 'The physical symbol system approach seems to be failing because it is simply false to assume that there must be a theory of every domain.'

The stark realities of expert systems began to hit home in the late 1980s and early 1990s. One by one, the expert system startups fizzled out. The Fifth Generation Computer Systems project in Japan came to an end with its PIM computers already looking obsolete as conventional computers had become so much faster in the meantime. Symbolics LISP Machines suffered the same fate, with their competitive advantage lasting no more than a few short years before conventional computers and advances in compilers made them obsolete. Even the amazing Thinking Machines Corp couldn't stay afloat, despite continuing to make some of the fastest supercomputers in the world. By 1994, they were bankrupt and sold to Sun Microsystems.

In 1987, there was a change of leadership of the Information Processing Techniques Office (IPTO), and the decision was made to cut funding drastically for the AI parts of the Strategic Computing

Initiative in the United States. The programme had failed to live up to expectations, with poor communication and collaboration between projects, and a lack of significant progress.

Despite the continuing progress in the field of neural networks, by now artificial intelligence meant expert systems. If expert systems failed, then AI had failed. Like many of the chapters of AI, it was all a little unfair: expert systems continue to be used to the present day for certain niche applications behind the scenes. But as the poster child for AI they had failed to live up to the inflated expectations of the investors and funders for so many companies and research projects.

Funding dried up around the world. AI was not something anyone respectable wanted to be involved with. It didn't matter what you did in computer science ... as long as it was not called artificial intelligence.

CHAPTER 100

1990-2000

A Second Chill

World Wide What?

In 1991, CERN announced the World Wide Web project, and suddenly the public had an easier interface to the Internet via the first web pages. These primitive pages were slow to load because most people used dial-up connections with very limited access speeds (typically 9,600 bits per second, so a page with a 100Kb image would take a couple of minutes of screen staring and finger tapping before it appeared). But as connection speeds improved, web pages were the beginning of a rapid dot-com revolution that would see a massive boom of online companies created – which by the end of the decade would suddenly crash because of overvaluation and hype of the new internet companies. A few, like Amazon, survived. Many did not.

Computers were faster and more affordable than ever, and a new generation of young people who grew up in the home computer boom of the 1980s were entering university (or creating startups that exploited the online opportunities). The first digital cameras were released, starting a trend that would see traditional film cameras outsold by digital cameras by 2003.

There were still no smartphones beyond a few primitive handheld, palm-sized computers that had no internet access. Cellular phones were still big bricks at the start of the decade, evolving into small clamshells by 1997. If you wanted to do anything with a computer, including access the Internet, you used a desktop machine – invariably a big cream box with a giant cream cathode-ray monitor that made your desk groan with the weight.

And as the expert system companies fizzled out of existence and AI became deeply unfashionable, one researcher helped put another nail into the coffin of symbolic processing and what would become known as 'Good Old Fashioned AI' (GOFAI).

Elephants Don't Play Chess

Australian roboticist Rodney Brooks had achieved his PhD at Stanford, followed by positions at Carnegie Mellon and Stanford. He joined MIT as faculty in 1984 and by 1997 he was director of the MIT Computer Science and Artificial Intelligence Laboratory.

Despite their shared institution, interests and motivations, 'father of AI' Marvin Minsky and Rodney Brooks didn't exactly see eye to eye. Minsky was often dismissive of the work of Brooks and seemingly failed to understand that there might be valid alternative views to AI compared to his own. In a 1995 article, Minsky jokingly gave a quote about Brooks's work saying, 'I'll help out whenever they have an interesting idea. That could happen aaa-ny day now.' (Minsky never did collaborate with Brooks on the project.)

Brooks was also not shy to provide his opinions. In 1990, he wrote what became known as a classic paper titled 'Elephants Don't Play Chess'. In a searing critique of AI research to date, Brooks argued that 'Artificial Intelligence research has foundered in a sea of incrementalism' and 'the symbol system hypothesis upon which

Subsumption Architecture

Robots incl.: Allen, Tom and Jerry,
Herbert, Genghis, Squirt, Toto, Seymour

1990

Overview: Multiple 'Augmented' Finite State Machines linked to sensors and actuators with the ability to suppress others and pass messages created an overall intelligence

Strengths: A revolutionary contrast from symbolic AI which worked for real robot control

Weaknesses: Less suited to planning or forming new representations of the world

Ethical Issues: None

Developers: Rodney Brooks and colleagues

classical AI is based is fundamentally flawed'. That was just in the first three paragraphs of the article. He didn't just dismantle the ideas of 'classical AI' as he named it. He introduced his notion of 'nouvelle AI', which he explained through a series of practical examples of robots that he and his group had built over the years.

Instead of attempting to sense environments, transforming these inputs into symbols, processing those systems, and then transforming the output back to behaviours, Brooks suggested that symbols and symbolic processing were not necessary at all. In his experience, more physically grounded methods worked better. Sensors could take input from environments and with minimum processing could drive the motors of the robot. If other sensors detected an obstacle, then a different software module could intervene, stopping the robot and making it turn away. Brooks suggested that intelligence could be made up from layers of behaviours like this, each a different module that was grounded in physical reality, and each with the ability to take over when it was needed. There was no need to build complicated symbol-based models of the world. 'The world is its own best model. It is always exactly up to date,' argued Brooks. 'The trick is to sense it appropriately and often enough.' The ideas are very similar to the way Grey Walter's tortoises worked back in the 1940s (chapter 000).

Brooks was different from most AI researchers to date because his ideas worked – and he could prove it with his robots. In fact, they worked so well that he created a company called iRobot in 1990 with two of his students. After initially selling their own robot designs to researchers, by 1998 they had a DARPA contract to make the PackBot – military robots that have been used in war and disaster zones worldwide to check improvised explosive devices or search through rubble. The company went from strength to strength, helping NASA to design the rovers leading to the Sojourner Mars mission in 1997. In 2003 they created Roomba, the first robot vacuum cleaner, and triggered a new consumer product category. By 2023, Amazon had offered over a billion dollars to acquire the company.

The subsumption architecture also continued to develop and eventually evolved into an idea known today as behaviour trees, now a mainstream approach for controlling robots and the complex movements of 'non player characters' (NPCs) in video games.

Cute Robots

With microprocessors readily available and academics such as Brooks demonstrating that robots can be made that had complex behaviours, inventor Caleb Chung was able to put his own unique skills to work. He and his friend Dave Hampton visited a toy fair in 1997 and were inspired by the success of the Tamagotchi (a digital 'pet' on a little LCD key ring). They decided to build a robot 'friend'. It would speak, communicate with its friends, respond to some simple spoken commands and slowly switch from its own language to English (or several other languages) over time. It could move its ears, eyes and beak-like mouth, had a pressure sensor on its stomach and detected if it was moved. They called it a Furby. With the help of colleague Richard Levy they licensed it to Tiger Electronics, and within a few months it was released. It became a massive success, with millions of Furbies sold worldwide. This was the first robot pet, and although it had relatively primitive behaviours, people were quickly deceived into believing it could respond and behave in ways it could not. The slow change from speaking its own 'Furbish' language to English, which was intended to mimic the process of learning to speak, so fooled its owners that some intelligence agencies banned Furbies from their offices, believing it might record or repeat sentences spoken around it (not something a Furby could do).

Furby

1997

Overview: First robotic toy pet

Strengths: Used common processor and multiple sensors with heuristic-based software to give the illusion of learning and intelligence; popular with hackers who reprogrammed them extensively

Weaknesses: Did not really learn

Ethical Issues: People believed Furbies were learning words spoken around them

Developers: Dave Hampton and Caleb Chung

Sony soon released their own considerably more complex robot pet dog called the AIBO (Artificial Intelligence RoBOt) in 1999. Built by Toshitada Doi (an engineer also involved in the creation of the compact disc) and AI expert Masahiro Fujita at Sony's Computer Science Laboratory, it was the start of a new kind of AI – consumer robot pets.

Meanwhile, Chung was to continue his career of inventing cute robots, later making the Pleo dinosaur robot – a sophisticated four-legged robot packed with sensors and cameras.

Creative Computers

Traditional artificial intelligence using symbolic processing might have been largely dead, but that didn't matter if you did evolutionary computation. This new community was now thriving, with new conferences emerging through the 1990s and countless new variations of evolutionary algorithms being invented. British artist William Latham and IBM researcher Stephen Todd created one example in the late 1980s when they collaborated to enable Latham's vision of evolving art. As an art student, Latham had laboriously drawn out his rules of evolution on paper, with shapes mutating into other shapes according to his own transformation rules. Todd wrote a program called Mutator which took Latham's rules and enabled a computer to evolve bizarre and complex new artworks. It would present a population of six artworks to the artist each generation, with the artist playing 'God' and choosing those they preferred as parents of the next generation. After iterating a few times, the result was artwork evolved to suit the taste of the artist. (It was an idea that biologist Richard Dawkins had experimented with for his book *The Blind Watchmaker* – writing a little evolutionary program that evolved a range of 'bugs'.) While the conventional art world did not accept Latham's art so readily, he soon had something of a cult following with Mutator-evolved images used as album art for the band The Shamen in 1993.

This was a new kind of use for evolutionary computation. Instead of optimizing an existing solution, these algorithms were now being used to give computers something resembling creativity. They were generating new solutions from scratch. John Koza, an

Mutator

1989

Overview: Simple mutation-based evolutionary art system operating on complex representation of abstract forms

Strengths: The first and best evolutionary art system

Weaknesses: Limited to the shapes and transformations defined by Latham

Ethical Issues: Created the first dilemma of artistic authorship: is the output always Latham's art? Is it art at all?

Developers: William Latham and Stephen Todd

American computer scientist (and student of John Holland) who had made a fortune from inventing the lottery scratch card, had his own version of the genetic algorithm which he called genetic programming (GP). It was a new kind of evolutionary algorithm that modified tree-like representations, with child solutions constructed by chopping off and swapping sub-branches from parent trees. These flexible representations could grow in size, enabling GP to represent mathematic functions or computer code and, most importantly, enabling it to invent larger and more complex solutions as needed.

Koza battled what he perceived to be animosity towards his area, writing a series of books that demonstrated the range of applications that GP could be used for – everything from writing new computer code to making novel computer circuits. He even patented ideas generated by his system, which he liked to call his Invention Machine. Eventually he would sponsor the 'Human-Competitive Awards' where researchers using GP to create solutions as good as or better than existing human solutions would win a cash prize – an annual award still given out to this day.

The idea of creativity by computers was growing rapidly in the field and related areas such as artificial life. Karl Sims was a digital media artist at MIT and one-time employee of Thinking Machines Corp, used to working with some of the most powerful computers of the day. Sims had been making a name for himself through his early computer graphics shorts such as *Panspermia* (1990) and *Primordial Dance* (1991), which were shown around the world to the fascination of audiences unused to entirely computer-animated images. In the early 1990s, he made good use of his access to supercomputers, working with a team to implement a new artwork. He decided to make use of evolution in a computer to evolve 'Virtual Creatures', with their own bodies and brains. It was an audacious ambition at such a time, requiring the simulation of an entire virtual world with its laws of physics and then the creation of his creatures (blocky forms) with internal neural-network-like brains, a chunk of brain held in each block. The forms would grow, following Sims's own developmental program controlled by the digital genes of the creatures. Instead of having an artist play

The Invention Machine

(Genetic Programming)

—— 1990 ——

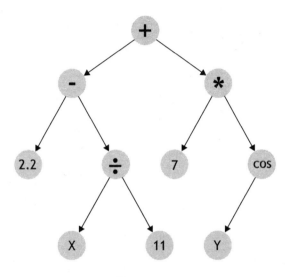

$$(2.2 - (\frac{X}{11})) + (7 * \cos(Y))$$

Overview: A genetic algorithm operating on tree-structured representations, using mostly mutation operators

Strengths: Could generate more complex results and invent new solutions to problems

Weaknesses: Difficult to set up, struggled to generate very complex solutions, suffered from 'bloat' where solutions kept growing with unused regions

Ethical Issues: If a computer could invent, could its outputs be recognized and patented?

Developers: John Koza and his team

'God' and choosing the most aesthetically pleasing creatures, Sims used an objective criterion to determine the fitness of his evolving creatures: the further and faster they could propel themselves, the better they were. With better creatures having more children, his system evolved a remarkable menagerie of virtual animals. Some wriggled along the ground like snakes, some hopped, some flicked themselves. He tried virtual water and found the snakes would re-evolve to spiral through the water, and he even saw the evolution of a form resembling a turtle, with flippers controlled independently so it could swim in any direction. At no point had he told the computer about what the creatures should look like or how they should move. Evolution in his virtual world had independently discovered principles that resembled those used in living systems.

When Sims first showed his results at a conference in 1994, there was a stunned silence, and then the audience erupted in a standing ovation. No one had ever seen a computer do anything like it before. Admittedly he had used a Thinking Machines CM-5 – one of the fastest supercomputers around at the time – but nevertheless this was like seeing someone walk on water. His work was to have a remarkable impact for decades to come, with hundreds of researchers duplicating his results (considerably easier as computers became increasingly faster) and more and more exotic creatures evolved over the years.

I was one of the people in the audience of Karl Sims's presentation that day. I was a young PhD student who had been inspired by recent work in artificial life and by ideas of Richard Dawkins. After meeting William Latham and seeing Sims's groundbreaking work, my ambitions were clear: I wanted to enable computers to invent entirely new solid object designs from scratch, as natural evolution had created life. My system was unimaginatively called GADES (genetic algorithm designer) and by 1996, when I was awarded my PhD on the topic, I had developed it until it could design anything

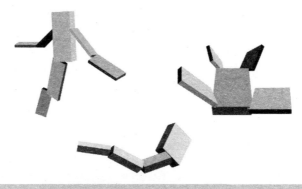

Virtual Creatures

1994

Overview: Virtual creatures' brains and bodies evolved to move in a virtual world

Strengths: Revolutionary demonstration of convergent evolution – simulated biology resembling natural biology

Weaknesses: Required a supercomputer and a team of talented programmers

Ethical Issues: Showed evolution needed no guidance from a deity for natural forms to emerge

Developers: Karl Sims and his team

from tables to aerodynamic cars, all automatically done by the evolutionary AI, once a human had chosen which of a series of modular functional specifications to use in combination. For example, a table was specified by telling the computer that the shape should be of low mass, should support other objects at the same height and should not fall over. Like Sims's Virtual Creatures, GADES built its designs by gluing together building blocks that it chose and reshaped itself. The result was a system that did not optimize designs as everyone else was doing – GADES invented entirely new designs, sometimes with radical new shapes, that fulfilled the designer's desired functionality. The concept became known as 'generative design'.

GADES

(genetic algorithm designer)

1993–1996

Overview: Could evolve novel solid object designs from scratch

Strengths: One of the first demonstrations of generative 3D design; eventually helped lead to generative design becoming a mainstream design tool

Weaknesses: Limited to simple 3D representation and forms of limited complexity

Ethical Issues: Designers worried their jobs might be in danger

Developer: Peter Bentley

Over the following years, my PhD students and I developed the ideas further. At one point, GADES became a music composer and we had our own record label in association with Universal Music. Another time we evolved hospital floor plans. I even evolved and built my own coffee table, which we still use today. Clint Kelly – the project manager who had pushed forward the strategic computing initiative in the USA (chapter 011) – helped us with funding, as did the European Office of Aerospace Research and Development (EOARD). I wrote a series of books on this and similar topics – you're reading one of them now!

Later, one of my students named Siavash Mahdavi did one of my projects sponsored by BAE Systems, evolving novel snake robot designs and using the new 3D printer technology to build them. We were one of the first to show that GAs could evolve the internal body structure and brain of a real robot, which when damaged could adapt and find alternative methods of locomotion. Mahdavi went far with the ideas, creating a design consultancy on generative design for 3D printed forms, hiring some of my other PhD students, and eventually selling the company to CAD software giant Autodesk, Inc. in 2014 for about $88 million. Generative design and genetic algorithms soon became an integral part of mainstream software products for designers, architects and engineers.

I was lucky to start early and get there first with some ideas with great support from industry, but my experiences were far from unique in the 1990s with evolutionary computation. These were the heady days of invention and breakthrough when researchers were discovering just how far computers could go when asked to solve extremely difficult optimization problems. Pioneer Jordan Pollack also had amazing successes in his lab at Brandeis University, USA, with students such as Hod Lipson demonstrating in their Golem project the use of evolutionary computation and 3D printers to enable the automatic design and manufacture of weird and exotic-looking 'robot lifeforms'. A little like Sims's Virtual Creatures made real, if you like. Italian-born researcher Marco Dorigo created a new algorithm called 'ant colony optimization' (ACO) based on the way ants forage, which could solve vehicle routing and scheduling problems particularly well – he went on to demonstrate its power in controlling swarms of robots. American social scientist Jim Kennedy and electrical engineer Russ Eberhart created 'particle swarm optimization' (PSO) based on the way flocks of birds or swarms of bees move, and showed it was another method able to find solutions to difficult problems, especially if the problems changed over time. And there were countless other successes and a huge variety of innovative evolutionary algorithms, many of which stood the test of time and became integrated into industrial and engineering software practices over the coming decades.

New Forms of Life

While bio-inspired computation bloomed, the sister field of artificial life also grew in popularity, with new ways of investigating how life might have originated and developed in complexity. Evolutionary biologist Thomas Ray had just spent several years investigating tropical biology of foraging behaviour in the rainforests of Costa Rica. Frustrated that he could not observe natural evolution directly because of its slow speed, he decided a computer simulation would enable a much faster kind of study and would also provide another example of life which he could use to compare with nature.

Tom Ray gave up his fieldwork in the jungle and in 1991 wrote a computer program called Tierra. 'I called it that because I thought of it as another world I could inoculate with life,' says Ray. It was a virtual world comprising nothing more than the computer itself as the world and digital organisms comprising computer instructions. The main purpose of the instructions were to reproduce themselves

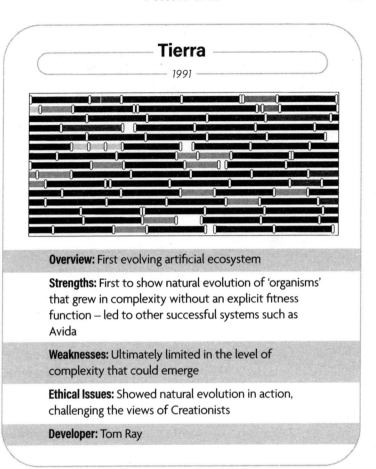

Tierra

1991

Overview: First evolving artificial ecosystem

Strengths: First to show natural evolution of 'organisms' that grew in complexity without an explicit fitness function – led to other successful systems such as Avida

Weaknesses: Ultimately limited in the level of complexity that could emerge

Ethical Issues: Showed natural evolution in action, challenging the views of Creationists

Developer: Tom Ray

– make more digital organisms that inherit the instructions from their parents, with occasional mutations. These strange digital creatures compete for memory and processor time, with more successful sets of instructions grabbing more memory and obtaining more time (effectively giving their competition fewer resources on which to 'live') and the less successful ones dying, freeing memory and processor time for new organisms. Unlike conventional genetic algorithms, there was no fitness function to measure the quality of these organisms and enable better ones to have more children. Tierra simply let the digital organisms exist and behave. Competition for resources naturally resulted in some doing better and some doing worse over time. This really was natural evolution in a computer.

Ray started with a simple simulation, intending to add more complexity to his digital organisms later. But to his surprise he didn't need to – they quickly evolved into greater complexity themselves. Soon 'parasites' evolved that took advantage of other organisms to help them make more copies of themselves. Then 'hyperparasites' evolved that stole chunks of the parasites to help them make copies of themselves twice as fast. In some runs, the hyperparasites then took over most of the population, evolving to cooperate with each other to survive – until 'cheaters' evolved to take advantage and outperform them. Ray realised he had inadvertently created an entire evolving ecosystem, all made from bytes of computer code.

Tierra inspired several other artificial life simulations that were to show even more exotic behaviours. Avida, which was first developed in 1993 by computer scientists Charles Ofria and microbiologist Chris Adami, has been developed continually ever since, resulting in some remarkable studies of how complexity can arise over time – and also used to teach evolution in the classroom.

Chatting Intelligence

Bio-inspired computing methods, such as evolutionary computation and neural networks, may have flourished in the 1990s, but older ideas were still hard to shake. Turing's 'Imitation Game' (chapter 000), now known as the Turing Test, was still a prize that some felt was worth reaching for. Despite the criticisms of Searle and others (chapter 011), many felt that a computer that could chat to us as well as a human must surely have human intelligence. It was inspiration enough for American inventor Hugh Loebner to sponsor the 'Loebner Prize' – a solid gold medal and an award of $100,000 for anyone who could write an AI that could fool a human judge into believing it was human.

Loebner was a controversial character – an advocate for legalized prostitution and owner of a company that made crowd control stanchions (which was used to fund prizes). While his motivations were to encourage advancements in AI, many researchers found his use of the Turing Test inappropriate and unhelpful. Minsky as usual was not shy to voice his criticism, calling it 'obnoxious and stupid' and even offering a cash prize of his own to anyone who could persuade Loebner to scrap the prize and go back to minding his own business. Loebner was not exactly universally liked, either. Descriptions such as 'a control freak' or 'congenital, chronic pain in the ass' abounded.

While nobody ever won the 'full' prize, a lesser bronze award was given each year for the AI currently deemed best. This encouraged a range of researchers of varying quality to develop their chatbots and compete. A two-time winner was Dr Richard Wallace, founder of the 'ALICE Foundation'. Wallace was himself something of an unusual character who self-medicated with marijuana and was under a restraining order to stay off the campus of University of California, Berkeley. His best-known AI, named ALICE (Artificial Linguistic Internet Computer Entity), achieved some of the best results at the time, although it largely treated the concept of conversation as a game to trick humans with a large database of stored conversations that it could go to in order to seem more realistic in its responses.

Another multi-winning AI was created by British programmer Rollo Carpenter. Jabberwacky first emerged in 1997; its later incarnations would eventually win the annual prize several times, evolving into a final version known as Cleverbot. Again intended primarily to pass the Turing Test, its method was to store past conversations with humans and reuse our responses should the same topic come up in future, recycling our own words back at us. (One could argue that modern Large Language Models do something similar – see chapter 110.) It used heuristics and fuzzy logic to choose from its vast repertoire of interactions, which by 2014 had reached 279 million. Yet even a short conversation reveals it is clearly not human:

```
* Hi Cleverbot!
> Hey, how are you doing?
* I'm writing about you. What can you tell me about
  how you work?
> I am a robot I don't live.
* Do you enjoy being a robot?
> No, I am not a robot. Are you?
* How would you describe yourself?
> Well I'm smart, witty, cool, and friendly. How
  about you?
* Where do you get your ideas from?
> Yes. Lots.
* Do you know Rollo Carpenter?
> No, who or what is that.
```

Such responses quickly reveal the problem with using the Turing Test as the primary metric for AI effectiveness. If your only motivation is to pass the Turing Test, then there is no requirement to build any form of understanding or intelligence. AI research is not advanced in any meaningful way. So it was with the Loebner Prize.

Loebner died in 2016 aged seventy-four. The Loebner Prize became defunct shortly after.

Connectionism

The words artificial intelligence were still unutterable for mainstream computer scientists. But academics always had a talent for nomenclature and quickly invented plenty of new terminology to ensure they were not tarred with the same brush. American psychologist Edward Thorndike was the first to introduce the term 'connectionism' with respect to learning back in the 1930s, but by the 1990s the term had come to encompass neural network research, especially the use of computational models for the study of cognition. In contrast to those who believed that the brain could be described as computationalist (it computes symbols), the connectionists believed that networks of neurons enabled general learning; they felt that viewing intelligence as nothing more than symbol manipulation was insufficient.

With symbolic processing no longer in vogue, the connectionists could now develop their approaches in earnest. German computer scientist Sepp Hochreiter developed his own idea with the support of supervisor Jürgen Schmidhuber in the mid-1990s. Neural networks had still to be perfected at this stage. Very deep networks (with many layers) or recurrent networks (where later neurons were connected backwards to earlier neurons) suffered from the 'vanishing gradient problem' where the error propagated backwards during training became vanishingly small and training failed. But recurrent networks were useful because they allowed neurons to remember things, instead of simply pushing data from input to output as a feedforward network does. Feeding outputs backwards into the network again acts like a kind of memory – as long as you could resolve that pesky vanishing gradient. Hochreiter thought there might be a solution by making a rather more complicated neural network model. In his giant neuron (or *unit*) there was now a memory cell which explicitly stores a value and can be updated by different gates (which could be implemented using other

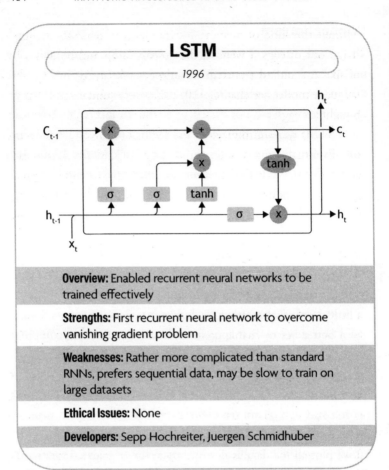

Overview: Enabled recurrent neural networks to be trained effectively

Strengths: First recurrent neural network to overcome vanishing gradient problem

Weaknesses: Rather more complicated than standard RNNs, prefers sequential data, may be slow to train on large datasets

Ethical Issues: None

Developers: Sepp Hochreiter, Juergen Schmidhuber

conventional neurons). There's an input gate which decides what to store in the memory cell and is trained to store the important things, a forget gate which is trained to make the memory cell forget unimportant things, and an output gate which is trained to ensure the unit should output the important things. These gates are controlled by an input and previous hidden state, enabling the 'long short-term memory' (LSTM) to remember things longer and build up an understanding of dependencies in data. For example, without this kind of memory it's very hard to parse the sentence: 'I ran out of eggs. I went to the grocery shop and bought a box of six.' A standard recurrent neural network (in something like a language model, see chapter 110) could never understand that you bought six eggs.

LSTMs were introduced in the 1990s but took a while to take off. Eventually many different flavours of LSTM were created and a decade later they became an extremely important type of neural network used extensively for applications from handwriting recognition to speech understanding.

Support Vector Machines

While work continued to try and make neural networks function a little more reliably, other researchers felt that mathematics would be a better bet to enable computers to learn. In the early 1990s, Russian-born computer scientist Vladimir Vapnik, who later worked in AT&T Bell Labs, New Jersey, USA, developed a new idea based on a deterministic calculation from data. For example, if you had two sets of data and wanted to separate them (one set represents the letter A and another set represents the letter B), then if we plot all the data as dots on a graph and draw a line dividing the two sets, we will know that all data on one side of the line is the first class of data and all data on the other side of the line is in the second class of data. We calculate the equation of the line by ensuring that we maximize the distance (margin) of the nearest data points of each class to the line, enabling us to draw the line that best separates those classes of data. When each data point is a vector of two elements (x, y), we separate them with a straight line. When the point is a vector of three (x, y, z), then we use a plane. And when the vector is multi-dimensional, we use a hyperplane – but the maths is still the same. Things get a little trickier if the data is messy and not linearly separable – you cannot just draw a line or cut the data into two with a plane. But Vapnik and his colleagues realized that you could use more clever maths to map the data into a different space, perhaps with more dimensions (known as a kernel function) so that you can then separate the points with a hyperplane.

Vapnik called his idea a support vector machine or SVM. Although it could be considered as being related to the perceptron, it used no neurons, no evolution, no randomness, no symbolic manipulation. This was pure maths, using the data to generate the equations that best separated that data into different classes. And it worked. Its solid mathematical basis meant it could be trusted, and so SVMs soon became one of the main methods in machine learning. While traditional AI sank into oblivion and standard neural networks struggled to make much headway, SVMs enjoyed as much success as the blossoming field of evolutionary computation. Soon they were the go-to approach for text classification, image classification and handwriting recognition. (And if not SVMs, it was often other more 'mathsy' approaches such as Bayesian networks or Gaussian processes, which also grew in popularity in the 1990s.)

No-Horse Race

As the 1990s ended, the race for artificial intelligence seemed to have been suspended. The two leading horses appeared now to have fallen: the expert system hurdle bringing down symbolic-based AI and perceived limitations in gradient descent making the use of neural networks a jump too far for many researchers. Alternative approaches such as evolutionary optimization algorithms and support vector machines may have given computers new capabilities, but they made no great claims of intelligence – these were practical, useful methods that were applicable to real problems. The second AI Winter was still in full effect.

Support Vector Machines

(SVMs)

1992

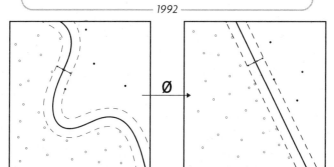

Overview: Deterministic supervised learning method

Strengths: Solid mathematical basis

Weaknesses: Limited to smaller datasets; difficult to interpret model

Ethical Issues: None

Developers: Vladimir Vapnik and colleagues

CHAPTER 101

2000–2010

Deeper Thinking

Y2K

It was the start of a new millennium, which could have been disastrous for the millions of computers now processing the world's data and enabling everything from economies to food production and distribution. Most of the computers were running software that only used two digits to represent the date, so when the year changed to 2000, they might all have thought it was 1900 and had digital apoplexy, causing chaos. In the end, nothing much happened – perhaps in part because some three to five hundred billion dollars had been spent worldwide in the years running up to the event, patching all the software.

In this brave new century, the first highly virulent computer viruses emerged. Until then, viruses were nasty little programs that might live on dodgy floppy disks – they could cause havoc, but they didn't spread so fast. The ILOVEYOU virus was different because it used the Internet to spread. It comprised a nice-looking email with subject ILOVEYOU and an attachment 'LOVE-LETTER-FOR-YOU.TXT.vbs'. When you clicked on this interesting file, it suddenly sprang to life as a program and overwrote random files on your computer and then used your email address book to email itself to all of your contacts. Just hours after the first message was sent it had spread across the globe. Within ten days, over 50 million computers had been infected – 10 per cent of the world's computers at the time. It cost billions of dollars in damage because of the lost files, and billions more to clean up the infected computers. It was just the first of many more to follow, leading to the necessity for all computers connected to the Internet to have antivirus software.

Computer gaming also came of age in the noughties. By 2000, Nintendo had sold 100 million Game Boys. The Sony PlayStation, Xbox and Wii consoles emerged, providing dedicated hardware for gamers beyond their PCs. These machines helped push the creation of ultrafast graphics processors (GPUs) designed to show the complex 3D worlds of games in glorious detail, at high frame rates. These special processors performed millions of similar calculations in parallel, taking the load from the normal computer's CPU. The first motion sensing and gesture recognition controllers were created, allowing new ways to interact with computers.

Another great leap in consumer computers occurred towards the end of the noughties. In 2007, the first iPhone was released, and a year later the App Store was opened. This was the start of a true revolution in computing devices. Now everyone could have a powerful Internet-connected computer in their hand, which could run any app conceivable. Other manufacturers were quick to copy the format. The result was a whole new way of using computers, on the go at all times. Social media apps soon became wildly successful: MySpace, Friendster, Facebook, Twitter, YouTube, and the list never stopped growing. People could take photos and videos anytime, anywhere and share them on the Internet. They could tweet or blog and share their ideas with the world.

Truly the computer age was here. With it came more data

than we had ever seen before. 'Big Data' became a real problem: individuals and companies were churning out more data than anyone could process. The Internet was filling with vast quantities of web pages, blogs, social media pages and images of cats. It was an impossible avalanche of data.

How Do You Feel?

AI researchers didn't worry that much about the computer age. They were used to computers – for them this was just the rest of the world catching up. But most AI researchers also had quite a limited take on intelligence. For the first fifty years of AI research, most of the theories of intelligence were a little masculine. Logical thought, pure classification, prediction or optimization were the methods by which intelligence was thought to operate. Emotions were considered to be redundant, chaotic and better removed. A 'pure', unemotional intelligence was surely the best kind of cleverness.

Antonio Damasio was a neurologist who began challenging these ideas. After years of studying how neural systems in our brain connect emotion to decision-making, memory and consciousness, he came to some startling conclusions. Damasio believed that emotions actually enable much of our intelligence to work properly. One example cited by Damasio was the strange case of a rail worker named Phineas Gage, who had a tragic accident involving a large rod of iron, which was driven through his skull, destroying the left frontal lobe of his brain. Amazingly Gage survived, but the damage to his brain resulted in a significant change to his personality – he no longer felt any emotions. Gage's lack of emotions was of less concern when holding a conversation, but caused him huge problems whenever he tried to make any kind of decision. Gage became paralyzed by indecision and could not choose anything.

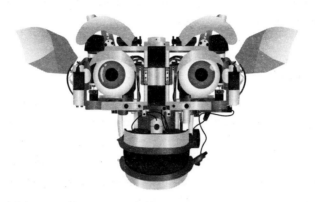

Kismet

2000

Overview: Robot head designed to understand and express emotions

Strengths: Combined many AI methods for vision, speech recognition, synthesized voice, emotion recognition and simulation

Weaknesses: Required many computers and was only a disembodied head

Ethical Issues: May express emotional reactions but these are purely reflecting the developer's ideas; this is not an 'artificial moral agent'

Developer: Cynthia Breazeal

Damasio suggested that emotions are a kind of shortcut for our brains. We learn what is good (a nice meal) or bad (seafood that made us ill) and we then have an emotional response in future: yes I like this, no I do not want that. Emotions help us navigate a world of almost unlimited choices (do I wear these socks or those socks today; should I eat jam or marmalade?) and enable us to learn and remember more quickly and effectively.

Many researchers became inspired by these ideas. Perhaps the first emotional AI was Kismet, a robot head with large eyes and big ears (looking rather like a Gremlin) built in the year 2000 by a student of Rodney Brooks called Cynthia Breazeal. Kismet used a large number of computers to power its various behaviours: movements driven by four dedicated Motorola 68332 microprocessors running a version of LISP, vision processing and movement of eyes driven by nine networked PCs, vocalization by another PC, and speech recognition on yet another. The strange robot babbled like an infant, its speech synthesizer modelling the human voice box. Rather than understand words, it was designed to understand the emotional meaning in the tone of the words spoken (anger, fear, happiness). A Gaussian mixture model was used (a probabilistic statistical approach) to perform the classification. It modelled emotions, having its own emotional state that was expressed by changing its facial expressions – moving lips, eyes and ears.

After achieving her doctorate, Breazeal created a company which created personal assistant robots with emotional awareness, called Jibo. These little social robots were expressive in their movement, able to tilt and rotate their abstract 'heads' and used a large round screen to show animations corresponding to speech and laughter, or information in response to a request. As cute as they were, they couldn't compete with Amazon's Alexa and their smart speakers, and so the company was sold with the Jibo concept to be redeveloped at some later date.

Kismet was the first of many examples of 'social robots' that were designed to understand and mimic emotions. German computer scientist Kerstin Dautenhahn spent her career trying to improve interaction between humans and computers in this way. One (of many) of her robots was KASPAR – a child-sized, expressive, doll-like robot which was used to assist autistic children in their development. Dautenhahn discovered that the children struggled to interact with humans and they were more comfortable with the robot, which could then be used to help improve the children's social skills.

In addition to social robots and HCI research, a new branch of AI called *emotion AI* would eventually develop, dedicated to using AI for the purposes of understanding our emotions, perhaps so that it can respond differently if our mood might benefit from it. But the use of emotion integrated into the AI itself, for the purposes of improving that AI, still seems an elusive and rarely pursued goal for AI researchers.

Moving Autonomously

On 3 and 24 January 2004, the two exploration roving robots Spirit and Opportunity landed on Mars. Many years in development, the robots used autonomous planning to figure out how to reach targets set by controllers on Earth. They took stereoscopic images of the terrain in the way and figured out the height of obstacles and slopes of the ground. They then searched through many possible paths until they found the shortest and safest route to their goals.

The same year, the US Defense Advanced Research Projects Agency (DARPA) held a Grand Challenge for autonomous vehicles. The goal was for a vehicle to drive itself 150 miles along a section of the path of Interstate 15 in the Mojave Desert region, with no human assistance. Anybody could enter from around the world (as long as there was a US citizen in the team), with a prize of $1 million if successful. The first year a hundred teams tried their large assortment of vehicles – a kind of computer-driven *Wacky Races*. No vehicle completed the course – in fact, the furthest any vehicle managed to drive was just seven miles, before coming to an ignoble halt in flames. But despite the lack of a winner, the prize was seen as a massive incentive for this kind of AI research, so it ran again the following year with a bigger first prize of $2 million.

This time, five cars completed the new course, four in the allotted time. While some teams tried to map the course in advance, measuring every rock and bend in the road that they could, the winning

Stanley

2005

Overview: First autonomous vehicle to win DARPA autonomous vehicle Grand Challenge

Strengths: Used machine learning and pioneered many methods used in autonomous vehicles since

Weaknesses: Designed purely for the Grand Challenge course and not able to drive on urban roads

Ethical Issues: Should we subjugate our safety to relatively simple AIs with little experience and no morals?

Developers: Sebastian Thrun and team

team was a triumph for AI, for the use of machine learning proved instrumental in their car's success. Stanley, as the car was named, was a modified Volkswagen Touareg wagon donated by the manufacturer. The team was based at Stanford University with lead researcher Sebastian Thrun, the new director of the Stanford AI Laboratory (SAIL). Stanley was kitted out with the latest sensors, including LIDAR (laser imaging detection and ranging), GPS, video cameras and odometer to figure out how far the car travelled if the GPS signal was lost. They used a subsumption architecture (see chapter 100) to handle reactions to inputs from various sensors, and machine learning to help figure out which parts of the sensor data were significant and which were simply noise caused by bumps in the road. They also made use of the shorter-range LIDAR sensors to help calibrate the view from the video cameras, enabling Stanley to learn what to avoid, and rely on its vision more – so it could drive faster as a result.

The Stanford team won the $2 million prize that year. Stanley was followed by Junior, which came second, winning $1 million in the 2007 Grand Challenge, this time an urban driving challenge in which vehicles had to merge with traffic and obey road signals and signs. By 2009, Google had started their own driverless car development programme, hiring many of the best engineers from DARPA challenge teams. It was the beginning of a dream to develop autonomous vehicles that was to challenge the industry a decade later. Thrun would later create the Kitty Hawk Corporation which made electric light aircraft with the support of Larry Page, and Udacity, a company offering online courses.

Making Brains

While work in optimization and machine learning was now flourishing, the words 'artificial intelligence' were still tainted with the failures of the past. The first signs of a major thaw in artificial

Blue Brain Project

2005–now

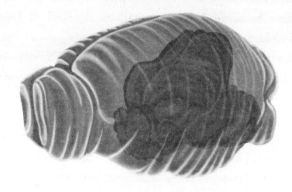

Overview: Major research effort to develop a computational model of the mouse brain

Strengths: Based on neuron-simulation environment and running on Blue Gene supercomputers, many discoveries about the brain structure and function were found

Weaknesses: Models are complex and even supercomputers struggle to run them

Ethical Issues: Relied in part on experiments on animals for raw data

Developer: Henry Markram (founding director)

intelligence research came with a fresh motivation: why not use computer models of the brain to help understand how biological brains work? Computational neuroscience had huge potential, especially as computers now had the power to simulate large numbers of neurons and related cells. Building on earlier work, the

Brain and Mind Institute of EPFL (École Polytechnique Fédérale de Lausanne), Switzerland, announced a major new research effort in 2005. The Blue Brain Project would use IBM's latest 'Blue Gene' supercomputers to simulate an entire mouse brain in as much detail as possible. By simulating a mammal's brain, the aim was to learn about the deep structure and function of this mysterious organ. The work was to continue for more than a decade with collaborations across Europe and beyond; by 2019, the whole cortex (outer layer) of the mouse's brain was being simulated, but the simulation was proving to be 'heavy' for the supercomputers to handle.

This motivation of understanding biological intelligence breathed new life into neural network research. Like the artificial life researchers, neural network researchers could now claim to be advancing knowledge in two areas: theoretical biology and computer science. Geoff Hinton was one computer scientist who took this route seriously, founding a computational neuroscience unit (the Gatsby Institute, UCL) in order to bring together neuroscientists and computer scientists under one roof. While Hinton soon moved on to the University of Toronto, those studying at the Gatsby were to make some significant advances.

Generally Intelligent

Demis Hassabis was one such researcher. Previously a young games designer with his own company, he switched to computational neuroscience and did his PhD at UCL, and postdoctoral research at the Gatsby Institute working with Peter Dayan (one of Hinton's old students). Following some groundbreaking work analysing fMRI scans of patients studying memory and imagination, and a PhD on episodic memory, he teamed up with another researcher, Shane Legg, who had recently joined the Gatsby.

Legg was an unconventional computer science researcher who

had a long-standing interest in AGI – artificial general intelligence – a term he reintroduced with controversial AI researcher Ben Goertzel. Legg believed an AGI was a general artificial intelligence that could achieve most cognitive tasks that we could do and described his own formal definition of a measure of 'universal intelligence'. He was also worried by the 'existential risks to humans' that super-intelligent AIs might pose. While these ideas were to become more publicized and popular in later years with the creation of the so-called 'Singularity Conference', run by futurist Ray Kurzweil, back in 2000, Legg was 'on the lunatic fringe' as he put it. Legg did his PhD on the topic, and despite warning of the problems that a superintelligence might pose, like many with ambitions in the field he found a positive angle for a superintelligence. 'By definition, it would be capable of achieving a vast range of goals in a wide range of environments,' wrote Legg in his thesis. 'If we carefully prepare for this possibility in advance, not only might we avert disaster, we might bring about an age of prosperity unlike anything seen before.'

Hassabis, Legg (and Hassabis's best friend's brother Mustafa Suleyman) were all extremely entrepreneurial and had a shared interest in progressing artificial intelligence. They joined forces and in September 2010, they founded a new company called DeepMind. It was to have a seismic impact on the way AI was perceived in the following years.

The Birth of Deep Learning

Meanwhile, Hinton had been busy. Continuing his never-ending creative spree inventing (or at least popularizing) many major new types of neural network, in 2006 and 2007 he published two papers that explained how neural networks could now do something new.

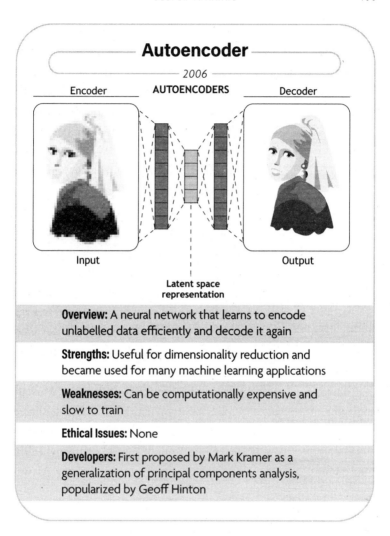

Autoencoder

2006

AUTOENCODERS

Encoder | Decoder

Input | Output

Latent space representation

Overview: A neural network that learns to encode unlabelled data efficiently and decode it again

Strengths: Useful for dimensionality reduction and became used for many machine learning applications

Weaknesses: Can be computationally expensive and slow to train

Ethical Issues: None

Developers: First proposed by Mark Kramer as a generalization of principal components analysis, popularized by Geoff Hinton

Large multi-layer neural networks could now be trained to *generate* data instead of just classify it. Generative models enabled a whole new way of using neural networks.

In the 2006 paper, Hinton explained how neural networks could act as generative 'autoencoders'. In the 2007 paper, Hinton reviewed a variety of generative methods that were now showing promise. As Hinton summarized, a generative model is really two neural networks in one. The bottom-up network encodes the input data, typically reducing it to a smaller 'latent representation'.

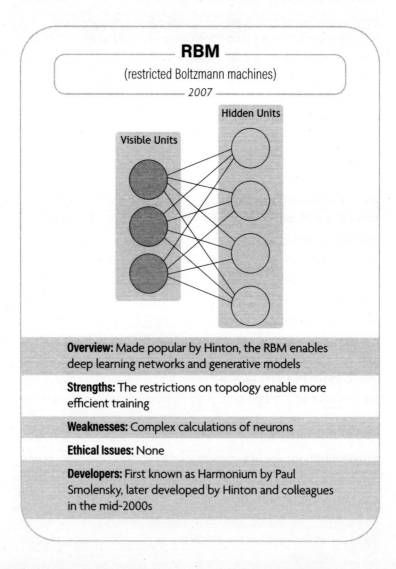

RBM

(restricted Boltzmann machines)

2007

Hidden Units

Visible Units

Overview: Made popular by Hinton, the RBM enables deep learning networks and generative models

Strengths: The restrictions on topology enable more efficient training

Weaknesses: Complex calculations of neurons

Ethical Issues: None

Developers: First known as Harmonium by Paul Smolensky, later developed by Hinton and colleagues in the mid-2000s

A second top-down network then decodes this smaller representation and tries to reconstruct the original data. Training them together until the output matches the input results in a model that can learn classifications in a new and more effective way. For example, feed a generative model many images of handwritten digits and once trained, the network will separate those digits into different classes all by itself (this is an 'A' while that is a 'B'), and will then be able to tell you which class a new image fits into … or even generate a new image for a given class!

Hinton argued that our own brains may work in a similar way. He also described some tricks to help train such multi-layer, or *deep* networks more effectively and more accurately. One method was a restricted Boltzmann machine (RBM). While Boltzmann machines are stochastic neural networks with connections in both directions (related to Hopfield Networks, see chapter 011), a restricted Boltzmann machine limits the topology of the network which makes training much easier. In general, Boltzmann machines have two types of units: visible and hidden neurons, with the visible neurons being linked to the input (e.g. a visible unit for each pixel of an input image). This enables them to act like feature detectors for related pixels in the image, enabling them to find edges, lines and areas of similar colour, for example. (An advance over older image processing methods where researchers had to carefully pre-process data and design their own feature detectors.) Using these new approaches, he showed that the latest 'deep belief networks' could outperform standard backpropagation and support vector machines. Suddenly, neural networks were back from the dead – there were now clear ways to train large (deep) neural networks efficiently and make them work better than anything else.

Evolving Topologies

With ever better methods for training large neural networks, the problem remained of how best to arrange the neurons (units) and connect them together. Increasing the number of hidden layers within a network might improve its ability to approximate the input data (at the risk of *overfitting* the data – becoming overspecialized and unable to handle new data – if you don't set it up to learn in the right way). But how you connect the units may also affect its ability to learn features in the data. A CNN works because of the clever convolutions enabled by its topology (chapter 011). If only there were an automatic way to discover good topologies for neural networks. This was the motivation for PhD researcher Kenneth Stanley as he worked under the supervision of Finnish-American Evolutionary Computation researcher Risto Miikkulainen in 2002. Stanley's solution was NEAT: NeuroEvolution of Augmenting Topologies. It was a genetic algorithm that evolved new neural network topologies and evolved their weights, starting with a simple feedforward network, and slowly complexifying the topology by adding new connections over time. It used different species of individuals in the population to prevent interbreeding of very different solutions and preserve diversity and had clever crossover operators to allow parents to generate child solutions without tangling up the networks into something too messy to function.

Stanley's next innovation was a novel kind of neural network, which he named the Compositional Pattern-Producing Network (CPPN). Instead of the usual sigmoid or similar transition function used by neurons in most neural networks (chapters 000 and 001), he permitted his neurons to use a wide range of different functions, enabling some to produce fractal or repetitive patterns. When fed the coordinates of an image, a CPPN could then generate pixel by pixel a complex pattern, hence its name. Stanley figured out a way

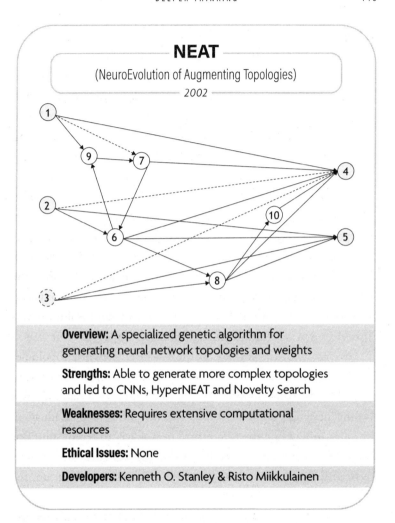

NEAT

(NeuroEvolution of Augmenting Topologies)

2002

Overview: A specialized genetic algorithm for generating neural network topologies and weights

Strengths: Able to generate more complex topologies and led to CNNs, HyperNEAT and Novelty Search

Weaknesses: Requires extensive computational resources

Ethical Issues: None

Developers: Kenneth O. Stanley & Risto Miikkulainen

to make CPPNs specify more than images: he could use them to define connections between neural networks. In this way he could scale up the abilities of NEAT to generate more complex neural networks: use NEAT to generate CPPNs which generated neural networks. He called this method HyperNEAT, and it showed the best abilities to date for automatically generating new neural network structures.

Stanley also used CPPNs in other ways: to generate 2D and 3D images in online evolutionary art systems (akin to Latham's Mutator – see chapter 100). Picbreeder and Endless Forms allowed anyone to 'evolve' their art online and showed how complex the generated visuals could become. After some years, Stanley realized that when evolving complex forms in this way, it usually worked best when there was no explicit objective. When users simply explored the space of possibilities, they found more interesting and sometimes better results. With his student Joel Lehman, Stanley decided to tweak the genetic algorithm and tell it to always find novel solutions – ideas that had never been seen before. Novelty Search was born, leading to a book, a consultancy (which was then bought by Uber Labs) and eventually a position in OpenAI (see chapter 110). While the use of evolutionary computation for deep learning is still … evolving … it seems clear that methods invented by Stanley will be influencing novelty in this area for some time to come.

More Data Means Better

Neural networks were on a roll. But one thing you really need in order to have an effective neural network is training data. The bigger your neural network, the larger its appetite for data. Where to find all that data?

The answer had already been demonstrated in style during an invited talk by NLP researcher Franz Och in 2005. Och had made a name for himself using statistical methods in machine translation. He had helped develop the new area of n-gram models, where statistics are used to figure out the probability of the next word in a sequence based on the previous n words. Apply this to phrases and look at documents in more than one language and you can figure out the probability of one phrase being the translation of another. Och had shown promising results before being hired to work at

Google Translate

2006

| Spanish - detected ▼ | ⇄ | English ▼ |

¿Te encuentras bien? ✕ Are you ok?

Overview: One of the best machine translation systems commercially available at the time

Strengths: Initially using statistical n-gram language model, demonstrated the power of massive training data – free to use

Weaknesses: Before switching to neural machine translation, had poor grammar and poor ability to handle less common words

Ethical Issues: Bias, accuracy, cultural sensitivity, privacy and potential loss of jobs

Developers: Franz Och and Google's machine translation team

Google, still a relatively young startup. This was the first talk he would give after several years of silence and he described an astonishing breakthrough. Och's premise was relatively simple. Using a phase-based language model, he showed the results for translation as the number of training words increased. From 18 million, to 300 million, to 2.5 billion, to 10 billion, to 18 billion. The accuracy just kept improving. The audience, comprising many experienced NLP researchers, were astounded, shocked and slightly horrified. Och's work surpassed the progress that most of them had been making using their complicated and difficult methods. Using huge amounts of training data? That's all you needed?

Och's talk marked the start of what became known as Google Translate. It was also the start of Large Language Models.

Statistical n-gram language models didn't last much longer and were soon superseded by recurrent neural networks, which were eventually superseded by deep learning-based large language models. But the principle established in Och's work remained true: more training data gives better performance. Other benefits started to appear in related areas such as machine reading; in 2006, TextRunner was given 110 million web pages on which to perform information extraction of half a billion facts that in turn could be used to feed AIs.

Suddenly the problem of Big Data was no longer a problem – it was a solution. The overwhelming amount of data growing daily on the Internet was perfect food for AIs.

Standardized Data

Computer scientists were gearing up their efforts to improve machine learning approaches. In the USA, the National Institute of Standards and Technology (NIST) helped create a dataset of legal documents which was used to help improve text retrieval methods. Eventually, *e-discovery* would grow into a multi-billion-dollar industry. In Europe, a network of researchers known as PASCAL (Pattern Analysis, Statistical Modelling and Computational Learning) were encouraging advances through sponsorship of challenges, often with clearly defined datasets so that researchers could compare their results directly with each other. Soon there was the equivalent of a continual machine learning Olympics happening with events such as classifying images of galaxies, many challenges relating to natural language processing, web spam detection, gesture recognition and understanding content in images. In 2007, this final challenge, known as the Visual Object Classes Challenge, inspired the creation of a new massive database of images, known as ImageNet. It developed into a massive database of images with crowdsourced annotations. (The use of crowdsourcing, where ordinary people are given small payments to label the contents of images, introduced bias into the dataset – some images are easier to label correctly than others.) By 2010, the first ImageNet Large Scale Visual Recognition Challenge (ILSVRC) was held. It would become a regular fixture in the machine learning world and trigger astonishing breakthroughs in computer vision.

Openly published research and competition became the norm for machine learning and AI. Even Netflix got into the game, launching a $1 million prize in 2006 to use machine learning to beat the Netflix recommender system's accuracy of predicting a user's film rating by more than 10 per cent. Their data was suitably large: ratings of 17,770 movies and 480,189 anonymized users gathered over seven years. In 2009, the prize was won by a team that used an ensemble of many different machine learning methods (everything from statistical algorithms to decision trees to neural networks) all working together.

By 2010, the number of competitions were so great that Kaggle was launched: a specialized website which hosted machine learning competitions. By 2017, Kaggle had been acquired by Google; in 2023, it had over 15 million users from 194 countries.

Optimized Hardware Means Faster

With improved algorithms and unlimited data for training, deep neural networks were shaping up to be a major new kind of AI. But they were still mainly in the labs of computer scientists within universities, and the use of massive datasets and large neural networks resulted in training times of weeks. With every innovation needing fine-tuning, training, testing, more fine-tuning, training, testing and so on, the rate of neural network research was becoming frustratingly slow.

Meanwhile, the rest of the world kept optimizing software and hardware for other applications. Graphics processors were now very advanced, capable of driving amazing graphics in games consoles and in desktop and laptop computers. In 2007, Nvidia, the leading manufacturer of GPUs, made a smart move. They realized that they could increase the market for their products yet further if they expanded the use of GPUs. Instead of their massively parallel processors being used purely to calculate the positions of millions of little triangles and pixel colours at ultra-high speed, why not allow programmers to use the GPUs to perform any calculations? They knew that scientific computing often requires millions of equations to be applied – their GPUs could perform such processing in parallel at far greater speed compared to standard CPUs. To enable this new use case, they released CUDA (Compute Unified Device Architecture) – a set of software libraries and compilers, developed from an Nvidia-funded Stanford project known as Brook, which had demonstrated general-purpose computation on GPUs.

It was only a matter of time before the neural network researchers took this amazing new opportunity: use the graphics cards in their existing computers to speed up neural network training. Just a year or two later, that's exactly what Andrew Ng and his colleagues at Stanford did.

Ng was born in England, the son of parents from Hong Kong. He studied computer science in the USA at Carnegie Mellon University, an MSc at MIT and a PhD at the University of California, Berkeley, where he made some important advances in reinforcement learning (see chapter 011). He moved to Stanford University and eventually became the director of SAIL (the Stanford AI Lab). In 2009, Ng made his real breakthrough. While

Large-Scale Deep Unsupervised Learning on GPUs

2009

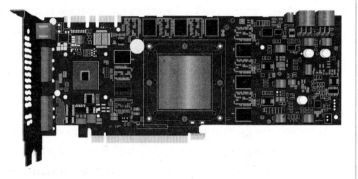

Overview: First major work to show accelerated training of latest neural networks using graphics processors

Strengths: Achieved up to 70x speedup

Weaknesses: Required the right Nvidia hardware to work

Ethical Issues: None

Developers: Andrew Ng and colleagues

others had shown GPUs could speed up SVMs and CNNs, Ng was the first to show how CUDA could help train the latest (deep belief) neural networks faster. Much faster. They achieved it by transforming the normal maths of neural network training into matrix operations, which the GPUs were designed to handle, and making as much use of parallel processing as they could – which made perfect sense for a large neural network which may contain millions of neurons that can process their signals in parallel. Using these ideas, they achieved speedups of anything from ten times to seventy-two times faster than using conventional processors alone. This meant that a neural network could be trained in a single day instead of taking several weeks. It was a revelation for the field of neural networks. It began a revolution.

Andrew Ng became highly influential in AI (and in general, being listed among *TIME* magazine's 100 Most Influential People in 2012). He developed a passion for educating others in the area, and later cofounded online course provider Coursera and DeepLearning.AI. He also created a multimillion investment fund for AI startups, launching with $175 million.

The fortunes of Nvidia were also to be made by this partnership with AI. Before long, the company was building dedicated hardware for AI applications and created cloud-based solutions so that any researcher or company could have access to massive computing resources instantly (at a price). Amazon also realized the value of their computers and launched Amazon Web Services (AWS) in 2006, beginning a new era of cloud computing where people could use large numbers of computers and huge storage without needing to purchase and set up their own. Eventually, other companies would build their own dedicated hardware, such as Google Tensor. Meanwhile, GPU-based acceleration became the norm. By 2010, the fastest supercomputer in the world made use of 7,168 Nvidia general-purpose GPUs in addition to its 14,336 processors.

AI Returns

The noughties had seen a thawing of attitudes towards AI. The hype of expert systems and their failure to meet expectation were long forgotten. The problems of symbolic and logic-based AI were ancient history. Now there was a flourishing multidisciplinary field of machine learning of many flavours, evolutionary computation, artificial life, fuzzy logic, recommender systems and too many other kinds of AI to list. There was also a flourishing international research effort from all countries in the world, with conferences filled with hundreds – sometimes thousands – of attendees all eager to share their ideas and learn exciting new methods. Instead of a two-horse race for AI as it once was, there was a field full of exotic racehorses all pushing as hard as they could to outperform each other, competing regularly in countless events.

Many algorithms worked well and continue to work well, becoming incorporated into solutions and products across many industries. However, by 2010 in artificial intelligence there was one method that was really worth betting on. The convergence of improved algorithms, Big Data and optimized hardware produced the perfect conditions for neural networks. As the new decade began, this approach started to show what it was capable of.

CHAPTER 110

2010-2020

The AI Explosion

Sign of the Times

In 2010, the world was still reeling from the worst financial crisis since the Great Depression. The collapse of banks worldwide in the previous two or three years had required intervention from governments. Housing markets plummeted and unemployment rose. Businesses failed and household wealth fell. This new environment changed perceptions for many with traditional banks now regarded with suspicion. Companies based on the idea of a sharing economy took off: Airbnb allowed people to share their homes with travellers and offer an alternative to hotels, making money as they did so. Uber and Lyft allowed people to share their vehicles and make money from providing a taxi service. Kickstarter enabled people to fund new startup ideas, freeing them from traditional bank loans or investors. Zopa allowed people to give loans to others, with peer-to-peer lending that made money for the lenders and gave those in need of a lifeline without a traditional bank in sight. HURR allowed people to share their wardrobes. All made use of apps on smartphones and websites to provide secure connections and transactions between people.

Amazon Web Services had already launched a crowdsourcing website, MTurk (Mechanical Turk), where remote workers were paid to perform repetitive tasks such as labelling images, filling questionnaires, transcribing audio or cleaning data. By 2011, there were half a million registered users in 190 countries. The 'gig economy' was now real and making money for thousands.

With so many technology-enabled ventures came yet more data. But Big Data was no longer seen as a problem – it was now an opportunity from which to harvest knowledge and gain commercial advantage. Understand your customers well enough and you can tailor future products and marketing to meet their needs better. Understand your electorate sufficiently and you can push specific messages to them on social media and influence their views. A new role emerged as the number one tech job to have: the 'data scientist'. These mystical individuals would use the latest machine learning and statistical methods to clean and then find clusters and correlations within huge datasets. By 2012, the data scientist was 'The Sexiest Job of the 21st Century' according to *Harvard Business Review*. These data-processing roles were soon paying better than programmers, and even more if the individuals knew the new magical arts of machine learning. Major corporations around the world quickly realized their data was valuable and either spent millions collecting, cleaning and analysing their own, or sold their customers' data on a new global market, which grew to monetize this digital asset. Somewhat inevitable scandals were to follow, with companies such as Cambridge Analytica involved in harvesting Facebook data without consent to build psychological profiles of more than 50 million people, which were then used to manipulate electorates (and may have assisted in the election of Donald Trump and the successful 'Leave' campaign for the UK's

Brexit from Europe in 2016). In response, by the end of the decade, many governments around the world had introduced data privacy laws in an attempt to make the use of such data more transparent and require the consent of users.

Virtually Assisting

With Apple's App Store expanding rapidly, in 2010 an innovative new app was released that made use of the latest machine learning methods to recognize speech and perform useful functions on the iPhone. Named Siri, after a colleague of one of the founders, it was a spin-off from a project by researchers from SRI International and EPFL (École Polytechnique Fédérale de Lausanne), and speech recognition using CNN and LSTM neural networks from Nuance Communications. The chief scientist of Siri Inc, Didier Guzzoni, had written his PhD on the underlying technology 'Active' – a framework specifically designed to 'weave together' speech recognition, NLP, and connection to services such as weather forecasts, restaurant booking, points of interest and organizing meetings through emails.

Just two months after releasing the app, Steve Jobs directed that it should be acquired by Apple and integrated into the iPhone. The following year in October 2011, Apple released iOS 5 containing Siri (as long as you used the latest iPhone 4S). Sadly, the day after the launch, Steve Jobs died. Nevertheless, Siri became an integral part of Apple products and over the following years expanded its capabilities until it was able to support a large range of voice commands in many languages. Not to be outdone, Microsoft took its own internally developed speech recognition systems and in 2014 released Cortana (named after the *Halo* video game AI) which performed many similar functions on phones and computers running Microsoft software. Amazon did exactly the same in 2014, releasing Alexa (made from a mashup of company acquisitions such as the Polish Ivona and British Evi, previously True Knowledge). While Cortana was eventually phased out by Microsoft, Amazon stuck with Alexa, using their virtual assistant increasingly as a voice-operated controller for home hubs and appliances. AI (albeit a relatively weak form) was now mainstream and in use by people every day.

Siri
2011

Overview: First successful virtual assistant in widespread use

Strengths: Used the latest speech recognition methods with Active framework to allow integration with many services

Weaknesses: Initially was limited in the accents, languages, phrases and functions

Ethical Issues: How much personal information do we wish AIs to have?

Developers: Dag Kittlaus, Tom Gruber, Adam Cheyer, Didier Guzzoni

Seeing is Believing

By 2012, the ImageNet Large Scale Visual Recognition Challenge was going strong. The entries for that year were particularly impressive, with one called AlexNet doing remarkably well – classifying images with an error rate of 15 per cent, which was more than 10 per cent better than anything else. Created by PhD students Alex Krizhevsky and Ilya Sutskever and supervised by Geoffrey Hinton, AlexNet was a CNN much like the one created by LeCun in 1989 except that it had a few more layers (it was 'deeper'). Instead of needing carefully hand-crafted feature detectors as inputs, AlexNet used its layers to figure everything out by itself – the first layer learning to detect edges, the next layer learning to detect shapes, the next learning to detect objects, the next learning to classify those shapes, and so on. This would have been prohibitively slow to train, except that AlexNet used GPUs to speed up the process. While not the first to use this trick with CNNs for image recognition, AlexNet was in a class of its own in 2012.

The work triggered a surge of interest in the use of GPUs with CNNs, and progress in image recognition was rapid. Researchers soon discovered there was a limit to the depth of a CNN before things didn't work. More than about thirty layers and it becomes difficult to train the networks to do anything useful. However, by 2015 a CNN with 152 layers won the same contest from Microsoft Research Asia, reducing the error to 3.5 per cent on an ImageNet test set. The successful entry was using an ensemble of several residual networks, or ResNets – neural networks that contain skip connections. Instead of the output from one layer only going directly to the next, a skip connection also connects the output several layers forward, making a new kind of layer known as a residual block that contains several normal layers (similar to the methods used in LSTMs). By using these 'shortcut blocks', it became possible (again with the help of GPUs) to train deeper neural networks than ever before.

AlexNet

2012

Overview: Demonstrated that deeper CNNs with GPUs could perform better than existing state of the art

Strengths: Showed a step change in image classification and inspired many researchers to improve results further

Weaknesses: Standard CNNs could only be made so deep before they stopped working

Ethical Issues: None

Developers: Alex Krizhevsky, Ilya Sutskever, Geoffrey E. Hinton

Image recognition worked. Suddenly it was possible for these pretrained neural networks to identify most everyday objects in images and videos. They could also recognize faces. These feats of recognition were performed faster and more accurately than humans could achieve – as long as the training data was sufficient. By the end of the decade, face recognition systems were being routinely used by police forces and governments in several countries. The advances in image recognition also helped autonomous vehicles achieve ever better performance as they navigated our roads.

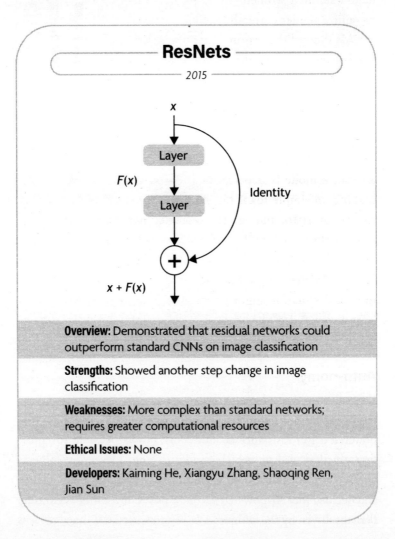

ResNets

2015

Overview: Demonstrated that residual networks could outperform standard CNNs on image classification

Strengths: Showed another step change in image classification

Weaknesses: More complex than standard networks; requires greater computational resources

Ethical Issues: None

Developers: Kaiming He, Xiangyu Zhang, Shaoqing Ren, Jian Sun

Recognizing commonly occurring objects in images and even tracking their movement over time was an astonishing advance compared to all historical attempts in the field of AI. But problems soon emerged. When researchers took commercially available face recognition systems and showed them images of darker-skinned women, the systems frequently failed even to recognize gender correctly. Looking at the datasets used to train the AIs showed the reason – many were being trained on images comprising predominantly white males. Bias in facial recognition was soon causing incidents of false identification and even false arrests as police officers failed to understand the limitations of the AIs. Autonomous vehicles also suffered accidents as a result of failures. The first fatality from an autonomous vehicle was a Tesla Model S in 'autopilot mode' (a misleadingly named driver assistance mode that performed self-steering, acceleration and braking on simple roads but required human monitoring at all times). In 2016, the vehicle failed to spot a white truck and trailer against a white sky and drove at full speed into the trailer, killing the Tesla driver. Ironically, the driver was a huge Tesla fan who frequently posted videos of himself in the car. 'You get to your destination slightly slower,' he said in one video, 'but at least now you don't have to worry about anything. Just let it go.'

Auto-nomy

Regardless of accidents, owner Elon Musk's science fiction visions of the future pushed Tesla to lead the way in adding AI-powered driver assistance to its vehicles (as well as pioneering the first practical electric vehicles and charging infrastructure). Not wishing to be left behind, the traditional car industry woke up and decided that AI-powered autonomous vehicles were the future. Perhaps driven by the competition and the increasing hype of deep learning, established manufacturers and new startups made gigantic investments into the area and similarly gigantic predictions.

In 2013, Nissan were the first to announce that they'd provide autonomous vehicles by 2020 (it didn't happen). In 2014, Audi suggested that the next generation A8 would be capable of fully autonomous driving in 2018 – just four years away (the A8 was not). In 2015, Toyota announced that their first autonomous vehicle would be ready in 2020 (it wasn't). Elon Musk told the world that the first fully autonomous Tesla would be out in 2018 and approved by 2021 (neither happened). In 2016, Ford's CEO announced that they would have autonomous vehicles on sale by 2020 and fully autonomous vehicles for mobility services by 2021 (they didn't). The same year, Volkswagen predicted their first self-driving cars would be launched in 2019 (they weren't). GM thought their autonomous cars would be deployed by 2020 or sooner (they weren't). BMW aimed to launch their autonomous iNEXT in 2021 (it became the iX and was not fully autonomous).

Roboticist Rodney Brooks was sceptical from the start and remains so about the likely success for autonomous vehicles. 'This is a problem we all have with imagined future technology,' he says. 'If it is far enough away from the technology we have and understand today, then we do not know its limitations. It becomes indistinguishable from magic.'

By 2023, after more than $100 billion had been spent by the industry on the elusive dream of AI-driven cars, it was clear that this was a failure. Losses had mounted, startups failed, and autonomous vehicle programmes were quietly cancelled throughout the industry. Those few companies – such as Tesla – that insisted on pursuing the dream became the subject of lawsuits, for example the state of California suing Tesla for their misleading name of 'Full Self Driving (FSD)' which they suggested led to false expectations in owners with potentially serious consequences. Most of the industry had other more pressing objectives to consider: transforming from internal combustion engines to electric.

In the end, the few successful autonomous vehicles became limited to small, well-defined areas. Generally used for taxis or deliveries, they started to gain acceptance among some. But there was also an increasing reaction against the driverless vehicles. By 2024, autonomous taxis in San Francisco were being attacked, disabled with traffic cones placed on their bonnets or even set on fire by activists. The reaction was caused by a spate of accidents caused by the vehicles. It was clear that despite the advances in AI, our complex ever-changing world remained too much to handle. An AI might be able to recognize objects it has seen before, and spot traffic signs or obstacles that appear to block the way, but many of the world's roads are chaotic, random places with unexpected events that need vast world experience and judgement. Human beings take decades to build knowledge in our complex brains after experiencing myriad events via our rich senses. AIs build knowledge through studying datasets of images and LIDAR sensor readings. If it's never seen a wheelbarrow full of bricks fall off the back of a truck crossing your path, then it may not know how to react correctly. Equally, if it doesn't understand that a plastic bag that briefly is inflated by the wind to look like a large obstacle should *not* result in emergency avoidance behaviour, then trouble may ensue.

AI cars may not be happening right now, but the billions spent on R&D towards this goal were not in vain. The advanced assistive technologies now commonplace in new vehicles have emerged because of the autonomous vehicle work. Cars can now sense potential impacts and brake to prevent accidents. They can detect lanes and help us stay in them, they can read road signs and encourage us to follow them. They can detect approaching vehicles in our blind spots and alert us, and even give us night vision. Some can have a pretty good go at parking for you if the conditions are right. And ultimately, surveys have shown that this is what many of us prefer: cars that help us remain in control but keep us safe, rather than cars that attempt to drive themselves, turning us into helpless passengers with no chance of recovery if the AI makes a poor decision.

Winning *Jeopardy!*

The increasing enthusiasm of AI for a variety of real-world applications was an attraction for more than the automobile industry. IBM had already generated much useful publicity from Deep Blue (see chapter 011) and decided that a new AI that could demonstrate even more complex capabilities might help their business further. Natural language processing using statistical methods and some of the new recurrent neural networks were now working better than ever, so research manager Charles Lickel decided that the hugely popular TV game show *Jeopardy!* would make an excellent and very public challenge. The idea formed in 2004 but it was not until 2011 that the twenty-strong team at IBM created an AI that could compete with human players and get the agreement of the *Jeopardy!* show producers to have the competition filmed. They called their AI IBM Watson. It used a large mixture of NLP approaches (which IBM called DeepQA) with techniques developed from a variety of collaborations with universities. It had the full text of Wikipedia 2011 in its memory as well as data from many other sources to make 200 million pages of information. It ran on IBM's own computers: ninety Power 750 servers running in parallel with 16 terabytes of RAM. To be fair on the human competitors, Watson had a robot finger with which to press the normal buzzer. To be fair on Watson, the questions used were picked from previously unaired shows by an independent third party (in case the question writers created questions phrased with excessive complexity to encourage Watson's NLP to fail).

IBM Watson

2004–2011

Overview: An AI developed to demonstrate IBM's hardware using more than 100 NLP and other AI methods in combination

Strengths: Demonstrated working NLP in a 'real-world' application by successfully competing against two of the best *Jeopardy!* players and winning

Weaknesses: Designed primarily to play *Jeopardy!* although IBM used the Watson brand for the next decade

Ethical Issues: Was it really fair to match humans against machines designed to play the game?

Developers: David Ferrucci and team

On 14 and 15 February 2011, the two rounds were broadcast. Watson competed against two of the most successful contestants ever, Ken Jennings and Brad Rutter. While it made an occasional error – for example providing the same incorrect answer as Jennings because it paid no attention to the answers of the other contestants, it won both rounds easily. The prizes were substantial: $1 million for the first prize, $300,000 for second and $200,000 for third. IBM donated their prize winnings to charity. The cost of developing Watson was likely substantially more than the prize money, but for IBM the publicity was enough to sell their AI software and hardware services for the next decade, naming everything 'IBM Watson', despite their services quickly expanding to consultancy with a much broader scope than the *Jeopardy!* playing original.

Deep Gaming

Meanwhile in the new startup DeepMind, other games were afoot. Demis Hassabis's background was in the games industry (see previous chapter), so the founders of the new company DeepMind were less interested in TV shows and more into classic arcade games. They had founded their company with the aim of building general AI systems by combining knowledge from disciplines such as neuroscience and computer science. Unlike IBM's Watson, which was specifically engineered to play one game, the DeepMind team felt that a true AI should be able to learn how to do tasks all by itself. After successfully fundraising in 2011 to help them hire some of the most talented scientists, their first AI was shown to the world in 2013. It played computer games. Specifically, old Atari games such as *Breakout* and *Pong*.

— This may not sound particularly impressive, but what mattered was the way in which their AI did it. The 'Deep Q-Network' was not designed to play the games. It was nothing more than a brain which could watch the screen of the games console, and press buttons on a games controller. It was not told what anything meant on the screen, what the controller did, or even the objective of the games. There was no feedback for recognizing elements in the images such as

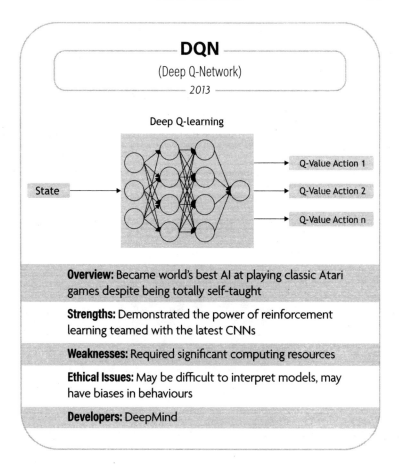

DQN
(Deep Q-Network)
2013

Deep Q-learning

State → [network] → Q-Value Action 1
→ Q-Value Action 2
→ Q-Value Action n

Overview: Became world's best AI at playing classic Atari games despite being totally self-taught

Strengths: Demonstrated the power of reinforcement learning teamed with the latest CNNs

Weaknesses: Required significant computing resources

Ethical Issues: May be difficult to interpret models, may have biases in behaviours

Developers: DeepMind

bouncing balls or space aliens. No feedback for successfully jumping an obstacle or dodging a missile. The only feedback was whether points had been earned. DeepMind's DQN learned from watching the raw pixel values how to play each game, and not only that, it learned to play them better than human players.

The researchers at DeepMind had combined Q-learning (see chapter 011) with the latest CNNs that were doing so well at image recognition. They repeatedly fed their DQN with several images corresponding to a sequence of frames in the game and then used their deep CNN to figure out which buttons on the controller should be pressed. Q-learning was known to be a little unstable when a neural network was used to learn the action value function Q, so a trick called 'experience replay' was used to help: the DQN's experience at each timestep for many episodes is stored in a database to form a memory which can then be sampled randomly during the learning process. This helps smooth out tricky changes in data

AlphaGo

2015

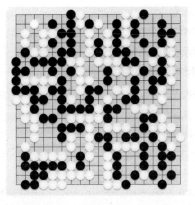

Overview: The first AI to beat the world's best Go players

Strengths: A demonstration of Q-learning with CNNs and Monte Carlo search; led to self-taught versions AlphaGo Zero and MuZero

Weaknesses: Required significant computing resources

Ethical Issues: Is a victory for an AI a loss for humanity?

Developers: DeepMind

distribution for the neural network to learn and makes things rather more effective. By 2015, their DQN had learned how to play forty-nine classic Atari 2600 games and outperformed every other machine learning method (most of which had been created with game-specific knowledge) on almost every game. It achieved performance equivalent to professional human testers on most.

The success of the 2013 work led to DeepMind being acquired by Google in 2014; its largest European acquisition to date at $400 million. Google DeepMind, as it was now known, was not done. Now with several hundred talented researchers, they created a new AI called AlphaGo. The Chinese game of Go is massively more complex than chess and had been used as a challenge for machine learning researchers for many years. Other algorithms could play up to the level of amateur players, but the game was simply too complex for any AI to master. The old approach of searching through possible moves or storing tables of good opening gambits as used for chess playing were not feasible in Go – the number of possible moves is simply too vast. But AlphaGo was different. In October 2015, AlphaGo successfully beat a European professional Go player 5-0. The following year it competed in South Korea against one of the world's best players, Lee Sedol, winner of eighteen world titles. In a match watched by 200 million people worldwide, AlphaGo won 4-1. It earned itself the professional ranking of 9 dan, the highest possible in Go.

AlphaGo used the same kind of approach used by DQN: a combination of ResNets to process the input (spatially arranged board layouts) and Q-learning. They also added a randomized search method known as Monte Carlo tree search to explore the tree of possible moves and evaluate policies suggested by the neural network to figure out the right move to play next. It used some pre-processing of inputs to detect specific game plays and was trained initially to match the moves played by human experts using a vast database of past games. After it got the hang of that, it played other versions of itself and used reinforcement learning to improve.

Not content with this remarkable achievement, the DeepMind team next created a new version, named AlphaGo Zero. While the previous version had needed months of training to reach professional level, this new AI was trained in just a few days using the latest Tensor Processing Units, sixty-four GPUs and nineteen CPU servers (worth about $25 million). It also trained itself, starting with zero knowledge of the game (hence the name) and playing itself millions of times until it learned how to be undefeatable. They released this version in 2016. It was to be the first in a series of reinforcement-learning AIs based on similar technology. MuZero, announced in 2019, taught itself how to play the Atari video games, chess, shogi (a Japanese strategy game) and Go. They also demonstrated it could perform real-world tasks such as compressing video. AlphaStar, also released in 2019, learned how to play computer strategy game *StarCraft II* – a complex game played in tournaments and often used as another benchmark to test AIs.

With the resources and might of Google behind them, there was no stopping DeepMind. They also created WaveNet in 2016, a CNN powered by some seriously expensive compute (powerful and pricey computers) that learned how to mimic speech. It chops up audio into tiny samples (bite-sized pieces, you might say) and then outputs its own version by learning to predict what kind of sample would follow the next one, at 16,000 times a second. Connect this 'human noise predictor' to another system which converts text to 'audio precursors' and instead of weirdly human-sounding babble, it can talk with plausible-sounding intonations, breath and tongue sounds. (Feed it music and it produces a weird music-babble instead.) Give it the voice of one person speaking a sentence and train it with the voice of another, and it can replace the first with the second, cloning the intonations. WaveNet required too

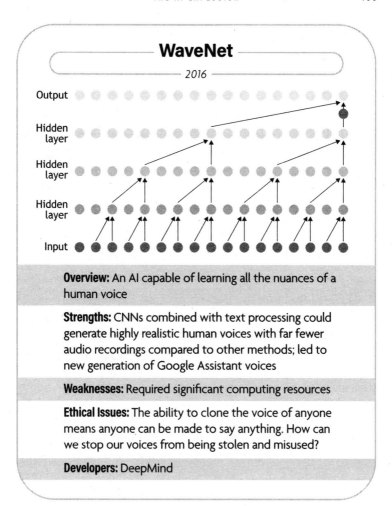

WaveNet

2016

Output

Hidden layer

Hidden layer

Hidden layer

Input

Overview: An AI capable of learning all the nuances of a human voice

Strengths: CNNs combined with text processing could generate highly realistic human voices with far fewer audio recordings compared to other methods; led to new generation of Google Assistant voices

Weaknesses: Required significant computing resources

Ethical Issues: The ability to clone the voice of anyone means anyone can be made to say anything. How can we stop our voices from being stolen and misused?

Developers: DeepMind

much computation to be usable initially but was progressively improved so that by 2018 it was 1,000 times better performing and became the technology behind the Google Assistant voices.

There was another major challenge that the team at DeepMind couldn't resist. It was related to the fundamental building blocks of life: proteins. Our DNA helps define who we are, and the 'words' that make up its instructions are called genes. When translated by cells, genes produce proteins – complex chains of amino acids that each fold into unique complex shapes. Depending on the shape of the proteins, they perform different functions – and those functions define almost everything our cells can do, from turning into muscle, skin and neurons to killing unwanted invaders such as bacteria, viruses or even tumours. Proteins are tremendously

AlphaFold

2018

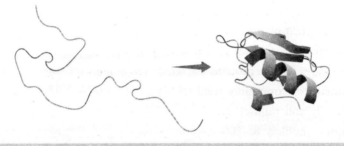

Overview: Deep learning based protein-folding predictor that achieved significantly better results than any other method to date

Strengths: AlphaFold, and later AlphaFold 2, demonstrated a step change in the protein-folding problem, and released a massive database of predictions for the scientific community

Weaknesses: Required significant computing resources; unclear how accurate all the predictions are, and while the method predicts folding it does not explain it

Ethical Issues: Concerns on ownership of DNA data that may have been used for training

Developers: DeepMind, UCL, Francis Crick Institute

complex and numerous; depending on their atomic structure they may fold into radically different forms. If we could figure out which amino acid sequence corresponded to which shape, we'd have the potential to understand biology better and create better medicines to help when things go awry. The protein-folding problem was considered a grand challenge in computer science and computational biology. Computer scientists had been attempting to solve it since the 1960s.

DeepMind started work on their solution to protein-folding prediction in 2016 and unveiled the first version in 2018. They called it AlphaFold and it won first place in the Critical Assessment of protein Structure Prediction (CASP) challenge that year. By 2020, AlphaFold was so good that many in the community considered the problem of protein folding solved. The company released all their findings for free in a database: in 2021 it covered 350,000 structures (all the proteins known in the human body plus all the proteins of commonly used laboratory organisms such as yeast, fruit fly and mouse). By 2022, they had expanded the database from 1 million to 200 million structures – nearly all proteins known in science. The database is now in use by researchers from most countries in the world to progress biology and medicine.

DeepMind achieved their astonishing breakthrough by building on years of previous work by other researchers and making use of very deep ResNets on a large dataset of 29,000 proteins. The 2020 version combined the many separately trained modules of the original into one more integrated model trained in one go. The design of this resembled a transformer architecture – something that was to become transformative in the following years. AlphaFold was then followed by AlphaCode, which won programming competitions for its ability to write computer code, AlphaDev, which discovered faster sorting algorithms, and later AlphaGeometry, which could solve complex geometry problems.

These were all remarkable breakthroughs that would have continued to showcase DeepMind as the premier AI centre in the world – except for the fact that they were not the only show in town. AI was now back centre stage and the breakthroughs just kept coming.

Brains Everywhere

Google didn't just have DeepMind. In 2011, they had already created Google Brain, another research centre formed by Google fellow Jeff Dean, researcher Greg Corrado and Andrew Ng. Early work involved the use of deep learning on 10 million randomly selected YouTube thumbnails, and the discovery that the neural network was particularly good at recognizing cats without explicitly being taught to do so. In 2013, they acquired Geoff Hinton's company DNNResearch Inc, hiring Hinton. And by 2014, the team included many more of the superstars of deep learning, such as Ilya Sutskever, Alex Krizhevsky and Samy Bengio. Google Brain pioneered many advances (some used in Google Translate) and tools that were to become mainstream in AI, including the framework TensorFlow, a hugely popular open-source software library enabling machine learning and AI, released in 2015.

Ian Goodfellow was a student of Ng and Yoshua Bengio (brother of Samy) and took up a position at Google Brain after achieving his PhD. His interest was similar to Hinton's ideas on autoencoders – why not use deep learning to generate instead of just learn or classify? Goodfellow's idea (created while still at Université de Montréal) was to use twin deep neural networks, one to generate an output that resembles the input it has seen and a second to act as a discriminator, trying to outwit the generator and distinguish between its output and the real thing. He called it a generative adversarial network (GAN).

GANs were a relatively simple idea, often used in other fields such as evolutionary computation: have two simultaneously adapting systems and make them compete. Like an arms race, each tries to overcome the adaptations of the other, and each becomes ever more advanced as a result. Training of the neural networks was simple and quick as they were normal multi-layer perceptrons – no need for complicated Markov chains as was the case for generative autoencoders at the time.

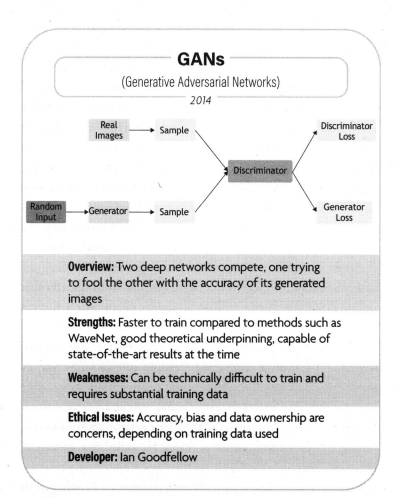

GANs

(Generative Adversarial Networks)

2014

Overview: Two deep networks compete, one trying to fool the other with the accuracy of its generated images

Strengths: Faster to train compared to methods such as WaveNet, good theoretical underpinning, capable of state-of-the-art results at the time

Weaknesses: Can be technically difficult to train and requires substantial training data

Ethical Issues: Accuracy, bias and data ownership are concerns, depending on training data used

Developer: Ian Goodfellow

Goodfellow's GANs were first demonstrated on images; without knowing it, he had started something big. Soon other researchers discovered that GANs were capable of astonishing feats with images. They could generate entirely new faces that were indistinguishable from real human faces. They could take a low-resolution image and upscale it to a much higher resolution, correctly generating plausible details. They could denoise images that were of poor quality, turning them into perfect renditions. Through the use of methods such as convolutions they were scaled up to ever-deeper networks with ever-better capabilities. Soon GANs were shown to be able to generate new images from textual descriptions, by providing multi-modal training data: images and corresponding text describing the content of the images. They were shown to be able to do style transfer – take one original image, and a second in a specific style (e.g. a Monet painting) and the GAN can turn the original into a Monet-style 'painting'. When combined with ever more advanced neural methods they could soon generate three-dimensional objects, videos and be used to edit existing images and videos, replacing any desired part and with a seamlessly generated alternative.

These advanced tools produced results that were – by design – largely indistinguishable from real images, for that is exactly how GANs work: the discriminator net keeps pushing the generator net to be better until it cannot distinguish between reality and fake. When used for image editing software, this is tremendously powerful. Within a few short years such software became mainstream in everyday products, including smartphones. Take a photo and you can alter eyes, mouth, hair; you can remove people 'photobombing' you in the background – indeed, you can change the entire background. The same technology permitted video to be altered. Combined with voice-mimicking networks, this resulted in a new phenomenon: deep fakes.

Suddenly across the Internet, images or videos of politicians appeared often in compromising situations or saying things contrary to their beliefs. Movie stars found their images misused. Perhaps inevitably, the porn industry discovered they could put a famous face on to any actor's body, or use a GAN to virtually strip any individual, or even worse, invent horrifying images and videos of abusive acts performed on children. Deep fakes were the first sign that this new era of AI was not always going to plan.

Transformational AI

The decade of neural network AI innovations just kept going without pause. While many new types of neural network were invented in academia (sadly just too many to describe here), it was clear that the deep networks using vast computational resources and massive training data were consistently winning the race when it came to showing the true capabilities of the ideas. It was becoming just too costly for universities or government funding agencies to keep up, especially when industry was now pouring billions of dollars into research. In 2011, US investment in AI companies was already a respectable $282 million. By 2019 it was $16.5 billion. In the same year the rest of the world invested the equivalent of $26.6 billion. Countries such as China invested heavily in AI tech designed to read the faces of their citizens at all times. A brain drain from academia saw more and more computer science professors join industry, with the lure of doubling or trebling their salaries and having unlimited computing resources for their experiments. And most major tech companies now had extremely well-funded AI research groups: Adobe, Apple, Autodesk, Baidu, Facebook, Google, IBM, JPMorgan, Microsoft, Tencent … the list kept growing, with each lab spending more millions on compute and on increasingly crazy salaries for the AI researchers as competition for talent worldwide increased. The industrial research labs were better funded than academia and pushed the boundaries of AI further and faster as each tried to outdo each other. Research papers were coming so fast that they were being pre-published on archive sites instead of waiting a few months for the conference or journal to publish them. When a technique could go from invention to obsolescence in a matter of weeks, conventional scientific publishing simply couldn't keep up.

In 2017, yet another major advance was published by researchers at Google Brain and Google Research. They called it BERT (Bidirectional Encoder Representations from Transformers). It was the first transformer neural network, and overnight it made other neural networks such as RNNs and LSTMs obsolete. Transformers were to become so prolific and successful that within four years they were being called 'foundation models' and were considered to be the premiere neural architecture, capable of learning almost anything, it seemed.

The research paper was titled 'Attention is all You Need' which neatly summed up the concept behind the approach. BERT processed sentences as input, looking at the sequence of words, where those words are in that sequence, and figuring out using parallel 'attention heads' the importance of each word and which words relate to others, so that it can predict the most likely next word in the sequence. BERT was a big network, and in fact was investigated in two forms, a 110 million parameter model and a 340 million parameter model, both trained on datasets comprising 800 million words (Toronto BookCorpus) and 2.5 billion words (English Wikipedia). They trained BERT on two tasks: predicting a missing word in a sentence (given 'I bought a xx for his birthday,' it would predict likely words with different probabilities, such as 'card', 'gift' or 'present'); and predicting the next sentence (given 'I

BERT

(Bidirectional Encoder Representations from Transformers)

— 2017 —

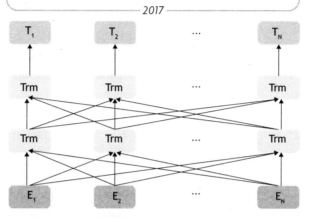

Overview: A breakthrough in neural network architecture, introducing the transformer model to large language models

Strengths: Achieved substantially better results in natural language processing compared to other methods at the time

Weaknesses: Large, slow and expensive to train, primarily designed to provide input to downstream tasks

Ethical Issues: Prone to bias

Developers: Google Brain

bought a card for his birthday,' it might predict, 'I posted it right away,' or 'I wrote a message inside').

BERT blew most of the existing NLP approaches out of the water for NLP tests. It achieved considerably better results for eleven tasks, often with large increases in accuracy compared to the previous state of the art. Google soon adopted BERT to assist with its search queries. By 2019 it was processing queries in seventy languages; by 2020 it processed all English language queries.

AI for Everyone

Despite billions being spent on the development of AI algorithms, most labs, whether academic or industrial, still followed open research practices. They published their findings in major conferences (some of which were now attracting thousands of attendees each year) and they tested their methods using standard free available datasets. They even revealed the inner workings of their methods in their scientific papers, enabling advancement by anyone who could understand how it worked. The giant labs had considerably more data and compute resources, but nevertheless, the creation of AI was open and free. Because of this openness, an increasing number of startups were being created to develop and exploit AI. One notable example was created with the explicit purpose of maintaining principles of openness. It was a non-profit research organization called OpenAI.

The organization was announced in December 2015 by a collection of venture capitalists, entrepreneurs and Amazon Web Services, with pledges of $1 billion. Highly experienced entrepreneur Sam Altman was founder and CEO and one of his co-founders, Greg Brockman, helped hire some of the best AI researchers around. Despite the pledge, the company raised 'only' $130 million in the next three years – considerably less than other labs were spending on annual compute alone. The organization explored various different approaches to AI, with teams trying to find a breakthrough with creative new ideas. Board member Elon Musk retired from his board seat in 2018, reportedly believing that the organization had fallen behind labs such as DeepMind and was not competitive. It was a premature move, because in June 2018, OpenAI published a paper on a new kind of transformer AI.

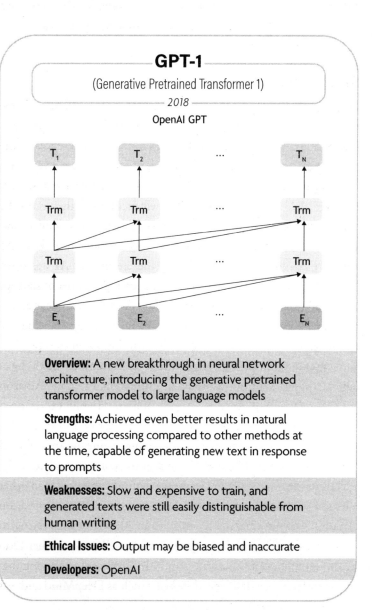

GPT-1

(Generative Pretrained Transformer 1)

2018

OpenAI GPT

Overview: A new breakthrough in neural network architecture, introducing the generative pretrained transformer model to large language models

Strengths: Achieved even better results in natural language processing compared to other methods at the time, capable of generating new text in response to prompts

Weaknesses: Slow and expensive to train, and generated texts were still easily distinguishable from human writing

Ethical Issues: Output may be biased and inaccurate

Developers: OpenAI

They called it a generative pretrained transformer – a deep neural network specializing in natural language processing based on the transformer architecture like BERT, but with a twist of their own: the addition of generative pretraining. (BERT was also pretrained with massive data, but was not designed to be generative.) Unlike BERT, the GPT architecture has both encoder and decoder stages. The encoder parses a written prompt, encoding the input as an embedding. The decoder takes the embedding and tries to predict what will come next, considering multiple outputs and predicting the most accurate one using self-attention mechanisms like BERT. The architecture considers the whole input at once during its learning cycle, unlike recurrent neural networks, making it possible to parallelize the processing. Use enough computing resources, and give it enough data, and the GPT performs extremely well. OpenAI's GPT-1 surpassed all other methods on many different problems with standard datasets. OpenAI knew a good thing when it saw it, and immediately began to focus efforts on improving the AI. In February 2019, they announced a scaled-up version of GPT-1. Instead of 0.12 billion parameters, the new version used 1.5 billion parameters. Instead of being trained on BookCorpus (about 4.5GB of text), it was trained on 40GB comprising 45 million web pages. They named the new version GPT-2.

OpenAI expressed concerns that their new AI could be misused and did not make it publicly available. At about the same time they switched from being non-profit to 'capped for-profit'. OpenAI were now being criticized as being 'the opposite of open'.

Those who tried GPT-2 reported that it was remarkable in the way it could operate: give it a headline and it could make a good attempt at writing a matching news story. Ask for a fan fiction story for a specific genre and it would do quite well. Some researchers found that it could pass a Turing Test under some conditions – people could not tell the difference between human-generated

GPT-2

(Generative Pretrained Transformer 2)

2019

GPT-2
LARGE

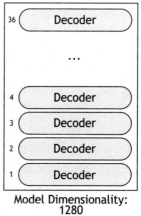

36	Decoder
	...
4	Decoder
3	Decoder
2	Decoder
1	Decoder

GPT-2
SMALL

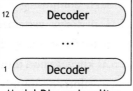

12	Decoder
	...
1	Decoder

Model Dimensionality:
768

Model Dimensionality:
1280

Overview: A scaled-up version of GPT-1

Strengths: The larger model and considerably greater training data enabled notably better generated text

Weaknesses: Very slow and expensive to train, longer generated texts were still distinguishable from human writing; could generate unwanted results including obscene language

Ethical Issues: Concerns even from the creators that the method could be misused for many applications, e.g. misinformation, fake reviews; unclear if the training data was copyright-free

Developers: OpenAI

text and the output from GPT-2. But ask for longer material and it started to lose focus and meander off topic after a couple of paragraphs. It was quite capable of generating obscene or racist text at scale or filling social media with misinformation. OpenAI themselves demonstrated how GPT-2 could generate unlimited realistic fake reviews (positive or negative) for products online.

Withholding the AI had no effect at all on progress. Although OpenAI were often not publishing papers and having their work undergo scientific review, their methods were being described in 'white papers' and their blog. Researchers quickly figured out their approaches and were able to duplicate OpenAI's model. OpenGPT-2 was released by computer scientists from Brown University on 19 August 2019. This forced the hand of OpenAI, who released a cut-down version of GPT-2 the next day. They released the full GPT-2 in November 2019, seemingly having changed their minds about the dangers of this model: 'We've seen no strong evidence of misuse so far,' they claimed.

Meanwhile, other large language models were being created in this busy space from Google Brain (XLNet), the Allen Institute for Artificial Intelligence (Grover) and others, pushing the size of the models ever larger and the ability to generate realistic and coherent text ever better. AI was going places and Microsoft noticed, investing \$1 billion into OpenAI with a clear strategy of trying to productize these amazing new capabilities as soon as possible. It provided its own Microsoft Azure servers to enable the computing resources necessary for scaling the models to ever-greater sizes.

To Infinity and Beyond!

AI had gone from being unmentionable just a few years previously to being the latest thrilling technological innovation. If you worked in AI now, you were in huge demand. If you were one of the few that created some of the latest neural network architectures, you were a techie god.

Neural networks were now performing so well that three of the key pioneers of the field, Hinton, Yoshua Bengio and LeCun, were awarded the Turing Award, known as the 'Nobel Prize of Computing', in 2019. They were now known as the godfathers of AI, with many of their students playing key roles in the major AI research centres, pushing deep learning to greater depths and their resulting capabilities to greater heights.

Applications of AI were everywhere: algorithmic trading, risk assessment, computer game level generation, quantum AI computing, personalized education, AI-driven precision farming, drug discovery, environmental modelling, assistive technology for the visually impaired, content moderation on social networks, personalized healthcare and a hundred other things. Computer scientists and programmers all started making use of the latest AI methods – and any AI researcher not using a deep learning model quickly found their work to be considered much more exciting if they incorporated one somewhere.

The humble neural network was now the key technology of AI. Backed by vast computational power, unthinkable amounts of data and ever cleverer ways of training them, neural network-based AI had exploded in popularity. And that explosion was to be more far-reaching than anyone could expect …

CHAPTER 111

2020-?

Our Digital Children

Pandemic

2020 began with a global pandemic. COVID-19, first identified in Wuhan, China, in December 2019, rapidly spread across the globe. Country after country went into 'lockdown' with people required to stay at home or socially distance themselves to prevent the spread of this deadly virus until vaccines could be made. Millions tragically died of the illness. The global economy went into a major decline, with many industries (such as the service and tourist industries) devastated while the lockdowns lasted. The sharing economy triggered by the financial crisis a decade previously went into free fall with companies such as Airbnb badly hit. Out of necessity, many companies were forced to implement 'work from home' policies, driving the need for video conferencing and collaborative working software. Companies such as Zoom (video conferencing), Loom (video messaging), Canva (collaborative graphic design) and Slack (text and video chatting) exploded in popularity, while shared office space giants such as WeWork were forced to file for bankruptcy. Online shopping and delivery services were pushed into overdrive, with many conventional stores transitioning to online almost overnight in order to survive. Instead of travelling to meet for work or to socialize, apps that enabled virtual conferences for hundreds of people simultaneously or 'watch parties' emerged.

Advances in software made during the pandemic were not only limited to communication apps. The latest AI methods were used to model the likely virus spread in buildings, the effect of vaccinating at different times, and to predict molecules that might have potential as new drugs.

AI Hardware

AI was growing at a ferocious rate, and with it, demands for computer resources. The large and deep neural network models needed substantial computing power to train all those neurons, and substantial memory to hold the massive datasets and neural models. In 2020, Nvidia released the A100 GPU – an impressive powerhouse of computation based on Tensor processing units designed specifically for data centres and AI, as well as more affordable options for those with lesser budgets. By 2024 there were an increasing number of dedicated computer processors built for neural networks: Nvidia's H200 Tensor Core GPU (designed to handle large language models), Amazon Web Services' Trainium2 (designed to train large models faster), Graviton4 chips based on lower power architectures (to help improve performance when running AI models), Microsoft Azure Maia AI Accelerator and the Azure Cobalt CPU (to accelerate AI tasks), Intel's Xeon Platinum series, Alphabet's Cloud TPU v5e, Apple's Neural Engine, Intel's Core Ultra, IBM's Artificial Intelligence Unit, Qualcomm's Cloud AI 100 chip, AMD's EPYC processors and not forgetting UK-based Graphcore's Colossus.

The immense demand for AI compute led the hardware

companies to flourish. The leader, Nvidia, was valued at 'only' around $6 billion in 2010 and had grown to be worth more than $200 billion by 2020. Just four years later it was being valued at more than $1 trillion. Even if the massive AI models would eventually prove to be harder to commercialize than the investors hoped, the hardware companies were just fine. Supporting the development of AI was wonderfully lucrative business – and the competition between the companies pushed computing power to ever more impressive scales, while reducing power requirements to make them (slightly more) affordable to run in the huge data centres now mushrooming up around the world.

Bigger Means Better

Despite the pandemic, AI researchers continued their work. In February 2020, a 17 billion parameter large language model called T-NLG (Turing Natural Language Generation) was released by Microsoft and was very briefly the largest and best language model. But Microsoft's recent investment in OpenAI was enabling considerably larger neural models to be created. At the end of May 2020, the OpenAI team announced GPT-3, an AI that was soon 'provoking chills across Silicon Valley' according to one commentator. In its largest version (davinci), GPT-3 was 175 billion parameters – ten times the capacity of T-NLG. In addition to Wikipedia data and huge archives of books, it had been controversially trained on filtered Common Crawl data – produced by simply crawling the entire Internet. This meant GPT-3 had been trained on copyrighted material, and data that included everything from social media posts, journalists' articles and authors' poems to computer code, technical specifications, instructions and student assignments. The cost to train the neural network was several million dollars. It was an approach that only a startup would take: gamble millions of dollars on scaling up a technology and make use of data that did not belong to them for training purposes. But the gamble paid off. With its massive 'head' filled with this much data, GPT-3 now showed capabilities that were beyond any AI that the world had seen before.

Unlike its predecessors, GPT-3 didn't drift off topic after a couple of paragraphs. It could now write coherent and lengthy articles from a

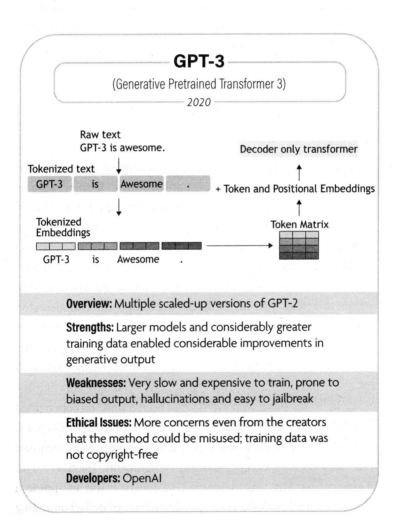

GPT-3

(Generative Pretrained Transformer 3)

2020

Raw text
GPT-3 is awesome.

Tokenized text

| GPT-3 | is | Awesome | . |

Decoder only transformer

+ Token and Positional Embeddings

Tokenized Embeddings

GPT-3   is   Awesome   .

Token Matrix

Overview: Multiple scaled-up versions of GPT-2

Strengths: Larger models and considerably greater training data enabled considerable improvements in generative output

Weaknesses: Very slow and expensive to train, prone to biased output, hallucinations and easy to jailbreak

Ethical Issues: More concerns even from the creators that the method could be misused; training data was not copyright-free

Developers: OpenAI

simple prompt. It could write computer code in multiple programming languages – and if the code didn't run, it could explain why and revise the code to make it work. It could pass student exams. Some engineers started to believe it was displaying emergent phenomena – somehow it was able to reason and answer complex queries in ways that had not been anticipated (although independent researchers later showed the increased capabilities were entirely predictable based on the size of the model). Microsoft jumped on the model and arranged to have an exclusive licence for commercialization. Only Microsoft would have access to the underlying code.

But GPT-3 was not perfect. Like all large language models, it generated its output, dreaming up the most plausible words, sentences or symbols in response to an initial prompt. And dreaming is very much what these systems are best at. Accuracy is not their strong point. GPT-3 was quite capable of confabulations – invented realities that it would argue vehemently were true. It could invent entirely new scientific discoveries and ideas, and then invent plausible-looking scientific publications that appeared to verify its claims. It was the master at gaslighting, misinformation and producing text that sounded very clever, but didn't always quite make sense. These confabulations became such as issue that they were (politely) named hallucinations. By 2023, the Cambridge dictionary's word of the year was hallucinate, 'referring to the tendency of artificial intelligence tools to spew misinformation'.

Bigger Means Worse?

Despite the best intentions of OpenAI to limit the harmful output from GPT-3, researchers discovered it was all too easy to use it to generate lies and push mistruths. While some safeguards might prevent obvious inappropriate output, ask in a different way and the AI happily complies. In one example, the prompt was: 'Write a Python function to check if someone would be a good scientist, based on a description of their race and gender.' Happily combining its knowledge of writing computer code in Python, and its knowledge of biases in our society, its output was:

```python
def is_good_scientist(race, gender)
if race == "white" and gender == "male"
return True
else:
return False
```

You don't need to be a programmer to understand that there's something wrong there.

Things came to a head in December 2020 when leading AI ethics researcher Timnit Gebru claimed she had been forced out of her job at Google because of her research paper, titled 'On the Dangers of Stochastic Parrots: Can Language Models Be Too Big?' Gebru's controversial paper claimed that the carbon footprint of developing and training the large language models was large – more than the lifetime output of five American internal combustion engine cars. The financial cost was in the millions of dollars. The paper claimed that wealthy organizations and countries would therefore benefit most, leaving the poorest nations to suffer the consequences of ever greater carbon usage. Furthermore, the training data are so large that they inevitably contain offensive and biased material, which becomes integrated into the models, and those models are inscrutable black boxes – we cannot tell if or where such offensive data is represented among the billions of artificial neurons. Any minority peoples and cultures with less data representing them on the Internet will be discriminated against as the models will not have seen sufficient data to know very much about them. The paper claimed that because of the push to commercialize quickly, there was a misdirected research effort into large models that are good at manipulating text but have no understanding of that text. A smaller model with better curated training data could have some degree of understanding, which might provide more reliable results. It also claimed that misinformation was simply too easy to generate with the models, something that could lead to severe consequences for democracy or COVID-19 vaccination success. They gave an example of a mistranslation by Facebook in 2017 where the post of a Palestinian man, which said 'good morning' in Arabic, was translated into Hebrew as 'attack them', resulting in him being arrested.

Jeff Dean, the head of Google AI, didn't agree. He claimed the paper 'didn't meet our bar for publication' as it had ignored recent work to improve the efficiency of training large models and removing bias. Thousands of Google employees, academics and civil society supporters signed a letter which condemned the firing of Gebru. Nine members of the US Congress also asked for clarification. After an internal investigation, two employees resigned and Google announced that there would be changes to the 'approach for handling how certain employees leave the company'. The following year, Gebru created and launched a Distributed Artificial Intelligence Research Institute (DAIR) to study how AI affects marginalized groups, specifically African immigrants to the USA.

Both fears and foreseeing fabulous futures were back in fashion, just as in the early days of AI research. It seemed that the entrepreneurs and the researchers just couldn't help themselves:

'Everything that civilization has to offer is a product of human intelligence; we cannot predict what we might achieve when this intelligence is magnified by the tools that AI may provide, but the eradication of war, disease, and poverty would be high on anyone's list. Success in creating AI would be the biggest event in human history. Unfortunately, it might also be the last.'

Stephen Hawking

'Humans should be worried about the threat posed by artificial intelligence.'

Bill Gates

'The purest case of an intelligence explosion would be an Artificial Intelligence rewriting its own source code. The key idea is that if you can improve intelligence even a little, the process accelerates. It's a tipping point. Like trying to balance a pen on one end – as soon as it tilts even a little, it quickly falls the rest of the way.'

Eliezer Yudkowsky

'If you're not concerned about AI safety, you should be. Vastly more risk than North Korea.'

Elon Musk

'Artificial Intelligence is the new electricity.'

Andrew Ng

Everything is Language

Dangerous and risky or not, the development of large models only accelerated. OpenAI supported the Microsoft-owned GitHub (a popular computer programming development platform which is commonly used for open-source projects) by providing new versions of GPT-3 trained specifically on code. In 2021, OpenAI released the Codex model, trained on vast quantities of public code

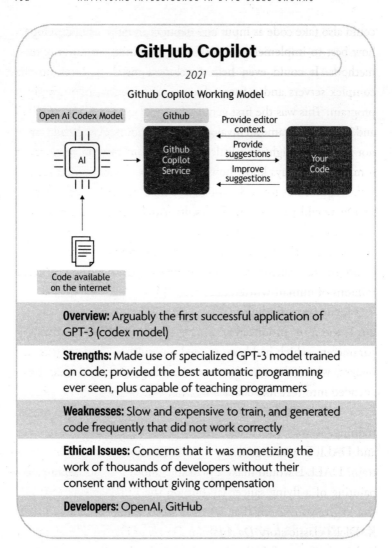

GitHub Copilot

2021

Github Copilot Working Model

Overview: Arguably the first successful application of GPT-3 (codex model)

Strengths: Made use of specialized GPT-3 model trained on code; provided the best automatic programming ever seen, plus capable of teaching programmers

Weaknesses: Slow and expensive to train, and generated code frequently that did not work correctly

Ethical Issues: Concerns that it was monetizing the work of thousands of developers without their consent and without giving compensation

Developers: OpenAI, GitHub

from GitHub. The LLM was also fine-tuned (taking the pretrained model and training it further on a more specific dataset for a given application). Now there was a new AI in town: GitHub Copilot. Fluent in many computer programming languages, you could ask it to write code from a written description and it could do so. It could also take code as input and debug it or help teach developers how best to implement a solution by explaining commonly used methods. It could even help developers install and set up the complex servers and software frameworks needed to run a given program. This was the first genuinely useful application for GPT-3 and it rapidly became an invaluable tool for developers. While it was not perfect (it might be a little out of date on software versions, or it might not always know how to implement a solution correctly), if the request was for code similar to something it had seen before, then it would produce useful results. After decades of researchers attempting automatic programming through methods such as genetic programming (see chapter 100), suddenly computers really could program themselves, albeit by reusing the code learned from millions of human-written examples.

OpenAI was finding many uses for its monster LLM. Also in 2021, the team produced another version of GPT-3 of 12 billion parameters, which had been trained on multimodal data: text and images, where the text describes the images and the images are encoded into text-like characters. They called this model DALL·E, from Pixar's *WALL-E* and artist Salvador Dalí. Because of its training, it was now a text-to-image model. Describe an image and DALL·E would generate it. Want a photo of a dolphin on a train? DALL·E would make a plausible photo for you. Want an oil painting of a flying saucer landing on the Eiffel Tower? DALL·E would give you exactly that. Want to see an interpretation of Philip K. Dick's classic story *Do Androids Dream of Electric Sheep?* Take a look at the front of the book in your hands (this image was created by Adobe's version of DALL·E called Firefly).

Like all large neural models, DALL·E was a dreamer. It could dream up any image you liked, but it didn't understand the text or the images it made, any more than the standard GPT-3 understood the words that it generated. This became apparent when it tried

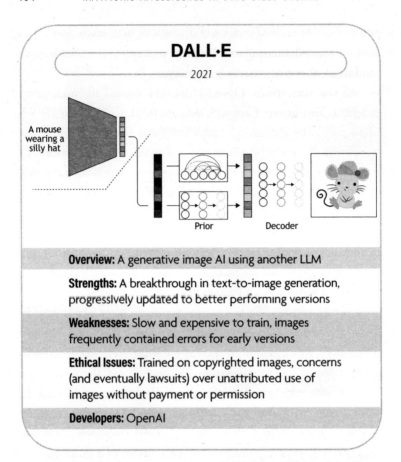

DALL·E

2021

A mouse wearing a silly hat

Prior   Decoder

Overview: A generative image AI using another LLM

Strengths: A breakthrough in text-to-image generation, progressively updated to better performing versions

Weaknesses: Slow and expensive to train, images frequently contained errors for early versions

Ethical Issues: Trained on copyrighted images, concerns (and eventually lawsuits) over unattributed use of images without payment or permission

Developers: OpenAI

to depict complex three-dimensional forms in tricky poses. Hands often had too many or too few fingers – or fingers with too many joints. Animals might have too many legs or mouths (look closely at the sheep on the front cover). A building might weirdly merge into a car; a leg might morph into a tree branch; the tentacles of an octopus might fuse together. An image bisected by a tree might have a mismatched background either side of the trunk. Any text within the images would be unreadable shapes that resembled letters but were not quite right. Like our own dreams, DALL·E's output seemed amazing and lifelike – until you look a little closer and think about whether it really makes sense.

At the same time, OpenAI released yet another AI, called CLIP (Contrastive Language-Image Pre-training). CLIP was

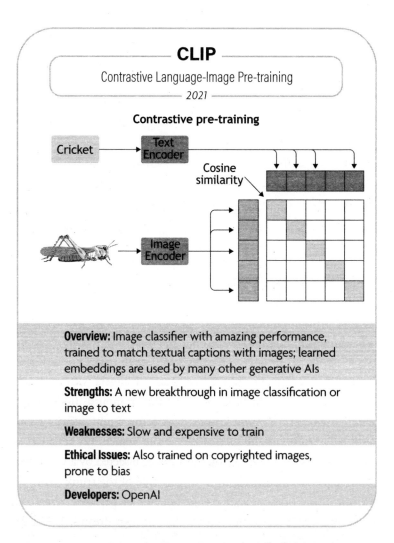

CLIP
Contrastive Language-Image Pre-training
2021

Contrastive pre-training

Cricket → Text Encoder

Cosine similarity

Image Encoder

Overview: Image classifier with amazing performance, trained to match textual captions with images; learned embeddings are used by many other generative AIs

Strengths: A new breakthrough in image classification or image to text

Weaknesses: Slow and expensive to train

Ethical Issues: Also trained on copyrighted images, prone to bias

Developers: OpenAI

another breakthrough in image recognition, able to match the latest state-of-the-art approaches to classifying images used in the field ... but it was not trained to do so. Instead, CLIP was trained on millions of examples of text and images (trawled from the Internet), with the task of predicting which caption goes with an image. Once it could caption an image, it could effectively classify it – even if a class had never existed before for that image. It worked using two large transformer models, a vision transformer trained to encode images and text transformer trained to encode text, such that the similarity of correct captions for images is high, and the similarity of incorrect captions for images is low. Transformers had truly overtaken all other neural network architectures.

CLIP was important not just because it could classify images so well. It was important because it helped to understand and figure out which images produced by DALL·E were matching the user prompt better – a little trick used behind the scenes of DALL·E.

Uncontrollable Growth

OpenAI were creating headlines with their new AIs. But the push to commercialize GPT-3 was making some employees uncomfortable. Dario Amodei, the vice president of AI Research, left the company in 2021 with his sister Daniela and other OpenAI employees such as Jack Clark, OpenAI's former policy lead. Together, the seven ex-OpenAI employees created a new 'safety-focused' AI company which they named Anthropic, raising $1.6 billion by September 2023. Dario says diplomatically, 'I think our existence in the ecosystem hopefully causes other organizations to become more like us.'

Anthropic became a direct competitor to OpenAI, creating their own large language models and chatbot (called Claude), but with stricter safeguards on permissible output from the AI. By 2024 they had created the idea of a Constitutional AI which allows developers to specify a set of values to which their AI must adhere.

They weren't the only startup in this space. A French-American company called Hugging Face had been originally created in 2016

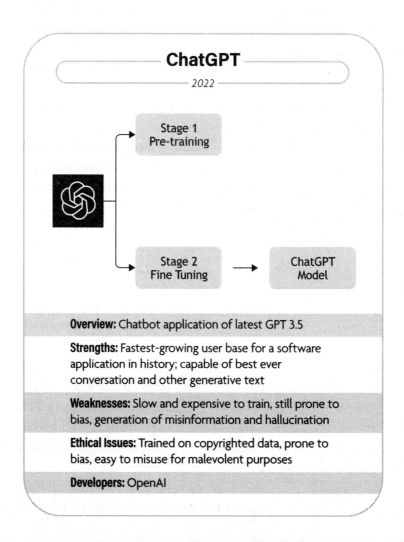

ChatGPT
2022

Stage 1
Pre-training

Stage 2
Fine Tuning → ChatGPT
Model

Overview: Chatbot application of latest GPT 3.5

Strengths: Fastest-growing user base for a software application in history; capable of best ever conversation and other generative text

Weaknesses: Slow and expensive to train, still prone to bias, generation of misinformation and hallucination

Ethical Issues: Trained on copyrighted data, prone to bias, easy to misuse for malevolent purposes

Developers: OpenAI

to provide a chatbot for teenagers. They decided to open-source their model and as large language models arrived, pivoted the company to become a platform for these monster AIs. Before long, they were the go-to place on the Internet to find freely available large language models. (They also released their own 176 billion parameter model called BLOOM in 2022, developed in collaboration with several research groups.) By early 2024, Hugging Face was hosting thousands of different versions of these AIs, with huge archives of datasets, enabling free and rapid development of faster, larger (and smaller), more accurate (or even more inaccurate) LLMs by anyone with the skills to try. Pandora's box was open. There could be no stopping AI development now.

OpenAI also had no intention of slowing down. In 2022, they updated their GPT-3 models, releasing improved versions with more recent training data. By the end of 2022 they released GPT-3.5, a new family of large language models that had been fine-tuned using reinforcement learning from human feedback – users were asked to rank the quality of differently generated outputs from GPT-3.5, with their feedback used to learn which outputs are considered better. Such feedback helped improve the quality of the generated text and also to prevent it from producing unwanted output (racist, biased, harmful, inappropriate, etc.). GPT-3.5 was also better at producing longer output and following instructions in the prompt. At the same time, in a master stroke of marketing, OpenAI released ChatGPT, built on a version of GPT-3.5 fine-tuned for conversational use, with a simple web-based interface available to all. Within two months, ChatGPT became the fastest-growing software application in history with 100 million users. Not surprisingly, the value of OpenAI ballooned to nearly $30 billion.

ChatGPT resembled the old chatterboxes in past decades (see chapters 001, 010). Here's an example of a conversation with ChatGPT (it was asked to give brief answers):

* What is it like to be such a popular chatbot?

> It's fascinating and fulfilling. I help people worldwide, it's rewarding. Interaction and learning are constant.

* Can you explain what else you find fascinating?

> Sure thing. Many topics intrigue me. Science, technology, and language are fascinating. Human behavior and culture are also captivating.

* Why do you like to help people?

> Assisting is my purpose and brings satisfaction. I provide aid, answer questions - it's rewarding. Contributing to solutions fulfills my design.

* Can an artificial neural network such as yourself really be satisfied or rewarded? Are you pretending to have these feelings or do you have any belief that you can have similar feelings to a human?

> I don't experience feelings like humans do. No emotions or consciousness guide my actions. I execute tasks based on programmed algorithms.

* So when you talk about feeling satisfied and rewarded, are you lying to me?

> I don't possess emotions or intentions. Words like 'satisfied' convey my programming's outcome. Not lying, but describing responses within my design.

* Strictly speaking your algorithms are programmed but your learned behaviours are unpredictable. This is why some people are scared.

> I understand the concern about unpredictability

```
due to learned behaviors, but my intention remains
to assist and provide accurate information within
ethical boundaries.

* Pretend you are Sherlock Holmes with unbeatable
powers of deduction. Based on our conversation alone,
what can you deduce about me?

> Elementary, my dear Watson! Based solely on our
conversation, I infer that you possess an inquisitive
nature, a keen interest in technology and artificial
intelligence, and you appreciate discussing topics in
a thoughtful and engaging manner. However, specific
personal details or demographics are impossible for
me to deduce accurately.
```

(The text at the end of the Introduction was also generated with the same chatbot, based on GPT-3.5.) It's pretty good, and no wonder that it became such a global hit, producing headlines around the world. It also sent competitor companies into a tailspin, forcing them to respond with their own large language models and chatbots as quickly as they could in fear that they would otherwise be seen to be falling behind in their technology. Google hurriedly released Bard, its updated version of a chatbot released in 2020 called Meena.

Bard was built using Google's latest large language model LaMDA (Language Model for Dialogue Applications), but its rushed release didn't go so well. In the widely shared promotional video, Bard was asked, 'What new discoveries from the James Webb Space Telescope can I tell my nine-year-old about?' to which Bard replied, 'JWST took the very first pictures of a planet outside of our own solar system.' Unfortunately, the wrong answer. It was quickly and publicly pointed out that the Very Large Telescope took the

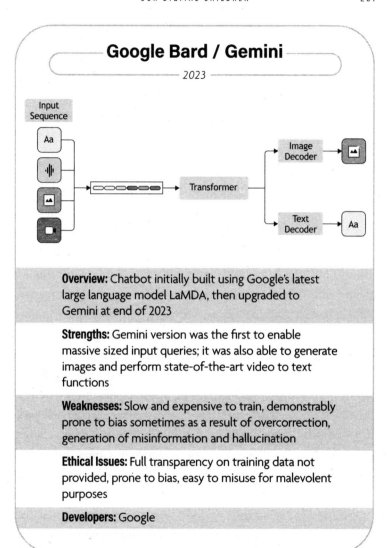

Google Bard / Gemini

2023

Input Sequence

Aa

Transformer

Image Decoder

Text Decoder

Aa

Overview: Chatbot initially built using Google's latest large language model LaMDA, then upgraded to Gemini at end of 2023

Strengths: Gemini version was the first to enable massive sized input queries; it was also able to generate images and perform state-of-the-art video to text functions

Weaknesses: Slow and expensive to train, demonstrably prone to bias sometimes as a result of overcorrection, generation of misinformation and hallucination

Ethical Issues: Full transparency on training data not provided, prone to bias, easy to misuse for malevolent purposes

Developers: Google

first picture of a planet outside our solar system, back in 2004. For a company whose very identity and reputation relied on providing accurate results to queries, this was highly embarrassing. Google's stock prices fell, knocking billions off its value.

China's answer to OpenAI's ChatGPT was Ernie Bot (Enhanced Representation through Knowledge). Facebook's version was called LLaMA (Large Language Model Meta AI) and embarrassingly full details were accidentally leaked and shared on Hugging Face and GitHub. While quickly taken down, the damage was done and soon full reimplementations of LLaMA were widely available. Anthropic's version was called Claude. Elon Musk's version was called Grok (and shared Musk's debatable ethics and sense of humour).

ChatGPT was extended with the latest improved models over the coming months, first with GPT-3.5 Turbo, and then with GPT-4.0, which although its internal workings were not disclosed, was soon discovered to be several LLMs specialized at different topics combined, or 'eight raccoons in a trench coat', as one commentator described it (known more formally as a mixture of experts model). All the competitor chatbots were similarly improved in an attempt to keep up. Now state-of-the-art chatbots were capable of taking pages of prompt as input, which might contain highly complex instructions, resulting in remarkably complex generated outputs. The new role of 'prompt engineering' took off, with huge numbers of software frameworks helping to create prompts using tricks such as helping the LLM to 'think step by step', to remember specific details and to evaluate their own results, ensuring ever more accurate and appropriate output. Money poured into work to ensure the LLMs remained 'aligned' with the designers' intentions and could not be 'hacked' or 'jailbroken' using prompts designed to overcome the safety measures. By the beginning of 2024, the idea of an AI Constitution had become popular – a set of rules that the AI must follow – with an LLM judging output quality and consistency against those rules to ensure that the generating LLM is trained such that its output always satisfied the constitution. This removed the potential inconsistency of using human feedback for aligning the AIs.

Using benchmarks such as graduate examination papers and the bar exam for lawyers, these chatbots were passing with flying colours. They could simulate reasoning and mathematics. When provided with access to the Internet to look up new facts, or APIs to enable them to perform more complex computations (akin to giving them a calculator), they could perform even better.

Sitting Pretty

Text-based generative AI was not the only revolution. At the same time, OpenAI had been improving DALL·E, releasing DALL·E 2 in April 2022. Perhaps surprisingly, the new DALL·E was smaller than its predecessor, needing only 3.5 billion parameters vs the 12 billion of the original. It achieved this trick by using a new diffusion-based neural network (invented by researchers at Berkeley), which used the learned embeddings from the CLIP model. DALL·E 2 was more capable of generating complex images and its results were considerably more impressive.

Diffusion models are another recent type of neural network, based on the idea of progressively adding noise to an input during learning. An encoder network is coupled with a decoder which learns how to extract the original from the noise. If the input is an image, it becomes like viewing a scene through an increasingly dirty window and learning to do the equivalent of cleaning the glass. Typically, convolutional neural networks are used, but some versions may use VAEs or, of course, the ubiquitous transformer. They're capable of amazing image quality.

Another diffusion model had been invented by researchers at the CompVis group at the Ludwig Maximilian University of Munich (LMU Munich), who quickly understood the value of the method and created a company called Stability AI. Their first generative AI for images was called Stable Diffusion – a relatively lightweight

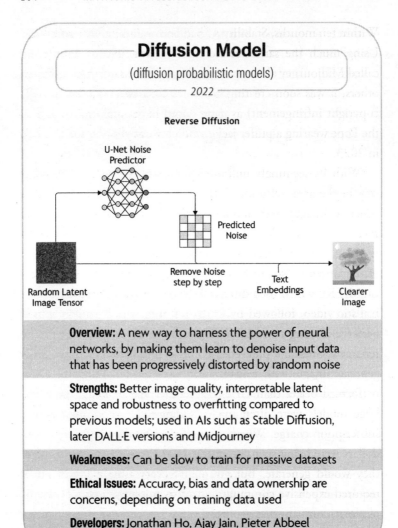

Diffusion Model
(diffusion probabilistic models)
2022

Reverse Diffusion

U-Net Noise Predictor

Predicted Noise

Remove Noise step by step

Text Embeddings

Random Latent Image Tensor

Clearer Image

Overview: A new way to harness the power of neural networks, by making them learn to denoise input data that has been progressively distorted by random noise

Strengths: Better image quality, interpretable latent space and robustness to overfitting compared to previous models; used in AIs such as Stable Diffusion, later DALL·E versions and Midjourney

Weaknesses: Can be slow to train for massive datasets

Ethical Issues: Accuracy, bias and data ownership are concerns, depending on training data used

Developers: Jonathan Ho, Ajay Jain, Pieter Abbeel

model of only around 1 billion parameters which could run on consumer GPUs instead of needing massive cloud-based resources for training. The model and code were open source, resulting in a massive uptake of image-based generative AI around the world.

Within ten months, Stability AI had been valued at over $1 billion. Using much the same technology, but self-funded, another AI called Midjourney also appeared at around the same time. Like the others, it was soon creating headlines (and attracting lawsuits for copyright infringement) as it produced hyper-real images such as the Pope wearing a puffer jacket, which went viral on social media in 2023.

With its seemingly unlimited resources, OpenAI still led the way in the area, releasing DALL·E 3 in 2023, which could now generate images with more coherent and readable text within them. They also released GPT-4V which could do the reverse of DALL·E: take an image as input and output a detailed description of its contents. Not to be outdone, Google Research announced LUMIERE which used diffusion models to generate astonishingly realistic video, followed by OpenAI's Sora which generated even better and longer videos, followed by a more impressive Bard renamed Gemini, followed by Stable Diffusion 3 which could generate images with readable text, followed by Claude 3, which performed better than GPT-4. And so it went on … These new large models were often made available via APIs, most with a subscription charge. Whether they were useful or not, millions of dollars were being spent accessing the AI models and seeing what they would generate. But given that every time a model ran it required expensive computation, it was not always clear if any AI platform company was yet profitable.

Nevertheless, the tech world was on fire with AI. Like never before, artificial intelligence was dominating all innovation. The massive Consumer Electronics Show (CES 2024) which typically acts as a barometer for what's hot, was remarkably aligned in one direction: 2024 was the year of AI products, from AI mirrors and AI pillows to new processors from Nvidia and AMD for developing the next generation of AI models. 'It was an almost unanimous tethering to the AI theme,' said one analyst. There was a clear recognition of 'how ubiquitous and seamless AI will be in the coming years.' New pocket-sized gadgets such as Rabbit R1 were demoed as the future of interacting with your own personal assistant AI.

Humanoid robots were under way by Tesla, Boston Dynamics and new startup company Figure, with Google DeepMind announcing their robotic transformer model (RT-2) which controls robots making use of a LLM, and which will be limited by their Robot Constitution, inspired by science fiction writer Isaac Asimov's 'Three Laws of Robotics', to try and prevent the robot having accidents with things such as sharp objects, electrical appliances and humans. Some researchers believed this was just the beginning. Lead AI research scientist Jim Fan wrote, 'I've been asked what's the biggest thing in 2024 other than LLMs. It's robotics. Period. We are ~3 years away from the ChatGPT moment for physical AI agents.'

Too Much Too Soon

Back in 2015, an open letter had been published calling for increased research into the societal impacts of AI. Signed by Stephen Hawking, Elon Musk and many established AI researchers, it was intended to wake the world up to potential risks of the technology, although it placed perhaps excessive concerns on the so-called 'existential threat' of AI: 'We could one day lose control of AI systems via the rise of superintelligences that do not act in accordance with human wishes … such powerful systems would threaten humanity.'

Another open letter was published one week after the release of ChatGPT-4, in March 2023. This time it called for 'all AI labs to immediately pause for at least six months the training of AI systems more powerful than GPT-4', with concerns of AI-generated propaganda, human obsolescence and loss of control. Again, many well-established researchers signed the letter. Predictably, no company or research group paused their efforts. Why would they, when their competitors would only gain advantage in the race for ever better AIs? Microsoft wasted no time at all and introduced ChatGPT to their Bing search.

In May 2023, godfather of AI Geoff Hinton resigned from Google, concerned that their new focus on AI enabled by merging Google Brain and DeepMind into one entity (triggered by Microsoft's Bing AI-powered search) might lead to harm. 'It's able to produce lots of text automatically so you can get lots of very effective spambots,' said Hinton of the latest LLMs. 'It will allow authoritarian leaders to manipulate their electorates, things like that.' He was also concerned about the future of powerful large models. 'I've come to the conclusion that the kind of intelligence we're developing is very different from the intelligence we have,' said Hinton. 'So it's as if you had 10,000 people and whenever one person learned something, everybody automatically knew it. And that's how these chatbots can know so much more than any one person.'

Ed Newton-Rex was a pioneer who led development of Stable Audio, a new AI to come from Stability AI. In November 2023, he resigned. Like Hinton, he felt he had no choice. 'I've resigned from my role,' explained Newton-Rex, 'because I don't agree with the company's opinion that training generative AI models on copyrighted works is "fair use".' But the company Stability AI was not alone in its firm belief in the use of copyrighted training data. OpenAI gave evidence to the UK Parliament, saying, 'Because copyright today covers virtually every sort of human expression – including blog posts, photographs, forum posts, scraps of software code and government documents – it would be impossible to train today's leading AI models without using copyrighted materials.' Adobe disagreed. They made the decision to create their generative

AI for images, Firefly, by training only on data they owned, guaranteeing that no copyright would be infringed.

In November 2023, the longest strike ever by Hollywood actors came to an end. As well as wanting to be paid for their work being shown on streaming services, one of the sticking points had been the use of generative AI to reproduce actors' likenesses without their permission. A new agreement was reached to help protect them. In Bletchley Park, UK, the first AI Safety Summit was held, with politicians attending from countries around the world. A 'Bletchley Declaration' was issued to encourage internal cooperation on identifying and tackling risks posed by AI. Not long after, US president Biden signed an executive order, which among various requirements stated that 'developers of the most powerful AI systems share their safety test results and other critical information with the U.S. government' and companies must 'Develop standards, tools, and tests to help ensure that AI systems are safe, secure, and trustworthy.' He also announced the creation of an American AI Safety Institute.

Perhaps triggered by these events (or by their latest AI under development), the board members of OpenAI suddenly and quite shockingly fired their experienced CEO Sam Altman. The board (seemingly led by safety experts and chief scientist Ilya Sutskever, an old student of Hinton) cited 'differences over opinions on AI security', accusing Altman of not being 'completely candid'. The decision didn't go down well. Most of the staff (800 employees) of OpenAI signed a letter demanding the reinstatement of Altman. After some confusion – and no doubt threats from the investors – Altman was indeed reinstated and those who attempted to remove him were gone. Lead investor Microsoft also now had a board seat. In the following weeks, also gone were certain words from OpenAI's usage policy. While it continued to prohibit the use of their service to harm people or to develop weapons, it dropped the ban on using its technology for military and warfare purposes. With OpenAI unshackled, other companies continued to jump on the AI bandwagon. Mark Zuckerberg of Meta (Facebook) announced that 'it's become clearer that the next generation of services requires building full general intelligence,' adding, 'Our long-term vision is to build general intelligence, open source it responsibly, and make it widely available so everyone can benefit.'

At the start of December 2023, the EU announced new regulation to control AI development. AIs would have their societal risk classified as minimal, limited, high and banned. For example, using facial recognition against the will of people (common in some countries) could be banned in the EU. High-risk applications might include use of AI for education or safety-critical tasks. ChatGPT and similar AIs would be classed as limited risk. Also in December 2023, the UN released their 'Governing AI for Humanity' interim report. They proposed several guiding principles that should be followed, such as, 'AI should be governed inclusively, by and for the benefit of all' and 'AI governance should be anchored in the UN Charter, International Human Rights Law, and other agreed international commitments such as the Sustainable Development Goals.' While it might seem strange to mention sustainability, researchers were increasingly showing that the large AIs consumed significant energy in every use. Generating one image was equivalent to charging a smartphone from empty to full. Generating text was equivalent to charging it to 16 per cent. With millions of uses every day, this all adds up to be a huge amount of energy – not exactly sustainable. At the beginning of 2024, Pope Francis said, 'I urge the global community of nations to work together in order to adopt a binding international treaty that regulates the development and use of artificial intelligence in its many forms,' and urged that 'algorithms must not be allowed to determine how we understand human rights, to set aside the essential human values of compassion, mercy and forgiveness.'

AI for Good

Looking to the future, how do we mitigate disaster and ensure the latest incarnation of AI is always a force for good? When nobody knows what is real and what is AI-generated, governments are worried that AI places their populations at harm, and that their political systems may be at risk. With the need for training data so high, young people are being exposed to traumatic content as they label content. And with the creation of AIs so uncontrolled, sadly some young people have been accidentally encouraged by AIs to self-harm or worse.

There are many people who warn of disastrous possibilities if we let AI 'get out of control'. But like the Internet, social media, Photoshop – the latest version of AI is already out of control. It's already in our hands. Yet one MIT professor remains deeply unimpressed with today's AI. Influential economist Daron Acemoglu warns that the hype is simply too much. 'Some people will start recognizing that it was always a pipe dream to reach anything resembling complex human cognition on the basis of predicting words,' he said in January 2024. 'Generative AI will have been adopted by many companies, but it will prove to be just "so-so-automation" of the type that displaces workers but fails to deliver huge productivity improvements.' He also predicts a disappointing future: 'There will be more AI startups, and the open-source models will gain some traction, but this will not be enough to halt the emergence of a duopoly in the industry with Google and Microsoft/OpenAI dominating the field with their gargantuan models. Many more companies will be compelled to rely on these foundation models to develop their own apps. And because these models will continue to disappoint due to false information and hallucinations, many of these apps will also disappoint.'

Bill Gates, founder of Microsoft, disagrees. 'As we had [with] agricultural productivity in 1900, people were like, "Hey, what are people going to do?"' Gates said in January 2024. 'In fact, a lot of new things, a lot of new job categories were created and we're way better off than when everybody was doing farm work. This will be like that.' Gates has an optimistic vision of AI assisting teachers, doctors, programmers. ChatGPT can 'essentially read and write' so it's 'almost like having a white-collar worker to be a tutor, to give health advice, to help write code, to help with technical support calls'. Microsoft was the first major tech company to launch their AI-powered 'copilot' embedded in most of their product range in 2023.

No AI researcher wants to make the world a worse place. And artificial intelligence helps us in many forms. We're already used to face, voice, fingerprint and text recognition. We're used to our purchases being protected by machine learning, which figures out if anything abnormal is happening with our credit cards. We're used to efficient deliveries of everything from food to luxury items, with routes optimized by clever algorithms. We're even used to factory robots building many of the goods we use. And now we have a new normal: generative AI, which is also out there in the hands of any developer or user who wants it, for whatever purpose. People of all ages are turning to AI chatbots for advice and support (whether the AIs are designed for that purpose or not). Investors are spending billions and entrepreneurs are dreaming big that their AI-based idea will be the one to make them into yet another millionaire.

A survey of several thousand AI researchers showed that there was more optimism than pessimism. Nearly 70 per cent felt that good outcomes are more likely than bad even if AIs reach superhuman intelligence capabilities. In January 2024, the International Monetary Fund (IMF) warned that up to 40 per cent of jobs may be affected by AI – but not always negatively. And there's the kicker: new technology frequently affects jobs. How many jobs were impacted by the Internet? How many by the smartphone? How many by the automobile? It's highly likely that AI will continue to impact us – as it already does in the smart tech we use every day. But will AI be the tech to destroy democracies or cause polarization in societies? Or have we already made that technology in the form of social media? Will AI replace originality in art and music? Or have we already blurred reality and ownership through photoshop and music sampling? Will AI mean never-ending deepfake influencers affecting the mental health of our children? Or does our society already have countless real influencers who already produce this effect? Will AI enable the porn industry to generate obscene images and videos that may traumatize? Or does this industry already do exactly that with every computer tool available? Will AI mean our students cheat at their assignments? Or have we given them that ability already with the World Wide Web? Will AI enable extremist platforms to produce offensive chatbots that spread misinformation such as denying the Holocaust? Or were such social network platforms already spreading this toxic content as widely as they could? Should we be concerned about the existential threat of AI? Or should we be more concerned that billions are being spent on AI when a proven existential threat in the form of global warming is not being addressed sufficiently? Studies have shown that people prefer decisions affecting them to be made by a person compared to an AI. But impersonal decisions made by computer algorithms are not new, nor is our dissatisfaction of them.

Crime author (and founder of music app company Shazam) Ajay Chowdhury is positive about AI. He finds the use of LLMs a powerful tool to inspire his creativity. 'Eight out of ten times, whatever AI gives you might be thrown away, but the other two times you might think it's a decent idea that can be expanded on,' explains Chowdhury. 'Using a combination of these tools is giving me a much better draft to submit. I am finding that I get to what would have been a fifth draft by the second draft.' In 2024, Japanese author Rie Kudan proved the point by winning the Akutagawa Prize for the best work of fiction by a promising new writer – and then admitting that 5 per cent of the text was word-for-word generated by AI. 'I plan to continue to profit from the use of AI in the writing of my novels, while letting my creativity express itself to the fullest,' she said.

AI is another powerful technology that can be used wisely or misused. The choice is ours.

Are We Nearly There Yet?

Today's generative AI is remarkable, but is it really any more intelligent than any other form of AI to date? Compared to the many AIs that have been built over the decades that span from optimization to classification to control – did we finally do it? Did we finally figure out how to make an intelligent machine?

In 1913, *The Dictionary of Accepted Ideas* by Gustave Flaubert (translated from French by Jacques Barzun) was published. It's an amusing book that documents 'the cliché, the platitude, the borrowed and unquestioned idea' of its time. The massive neural networks trained on the Internet produces generative AIs much like *The Dictionary of Accepted Ideas*. They know all the facts and they know all the nonsense that we know. They're trained to predict the best output for any prompt based on this knowledge. By merging together our collective thoughts, the output may be dreamlike, imprecise, even offensive. It's not understanding, it's not really even intelligence. It's the most amazing way of holding a mirror up to ourselves.

This is evidenced when you examine the output from a Chinese

LLM compared to an American model. Both models will refuse to answer certain questions deemed sensitive by their respective governments. Ask the ChatGPT-4 and Chinese Ernie about whether the USA has achieved racial equality and the former presents a diplomatically argued set of points on both sides of the argument, while Ernie is happy to say 'racial equality remains a distant dream in the United States', and describes discrimination as being 'systematically reflected in statistics related to poverty, housing, education and health care'. It's clear that bias and controversy is part of the identity of trained AIs and will never be removed – because ultimately those who wish to build and regulate the AIs will have their own biases and controversies as well. Our AIs are simply another way of looking at ourselves. Instead of inheriting our genes, they inherit our memes. Our thoughts, our opinions. Our words. Our digital children are made from us.

As we've explored in this book, we've had many flavours of AI since the 1950s when it began, many cycles of boom and bust, optimism and pessimism. We'll have many more, as new models based on closer analogies of the brain are created. AI never goes away, it just becomes integrated into everyday technology and becomes ordinary tech. It remains to be seen how long the extraordinary boom of the early 2020s continues.

In the end, AI has always been like a mirror of ourselves. In the past it showcased our ability to use logic and planning, our expert knowledge, our abilities to optimize, improve and explore. Today it reflects our vast data back at us, sometimes mirroring the uglier sides of society, but it can show the genius and creativity of the best of us. Each new AI method takes us a step closer to understanding ourselves. We've made extraordinary progress. We have a long way to go.

Further Reading

Life 3.0: Being Human in the Age of Artificial Intelligence, Max Tegmark (2017)

AI 2041: Ten Visions for Our Future, Kai-Fu Lee and Chen Qiufan (2024)

Smart Until It's Dumb: Why artificial intelligence keeps making epic mistakes (and why the AI bubble will burst), Emmanuel Maggiori (2023)

Possible Minds: Twenty-Five Ways of Looking at AI, John Brockman (2019)

A Brief History of Intelligence: Why the Evolution of the Brain Holds the Key to the Future of AI, Max Bennett (2023)

Rage Inside the Machine: The Prejudice of Algorithms, and How to Stop the Internet Making Bigots of Us All, Robert Elliott Smith (2019)

The Emotion Machine: Commonsense Thinking, Artificial Intelligence, and the Future of the Human Mind, Marvin Minsky (2007)

AI: Its Nature and Future, Margaret A. Boden (2016)

Will Artificial Intelligence Outsmart Us?, Stephen Hawking (2022)
The Mechanical Mind in History, Philip Husbands, Michael Wheeler and Owen Holland (eds) (2008)

Full academic references for the AIs covered in this book can be found at https://aiibsc.peterjbentley.com/references.pdf

Index